Carolina Cooks

Favorite Main Dishes, Vegetables, *and*
Much More *from the* Old North State

FOY ALLEN EDELMAN

Manufactured in the
United States of America
Designed and set by
Brad Goodwin

Photo of the author on
the back cover is by Susan
Carson. Photographs of Inez
Blackwell, Retha Durham,
Ellaree Everhart, Jennie
and Jim Vance were taken
by Anne Phillips. All other
photographs were taken by
the author.

The paper in this book meets the guidelines for
permanence and durability of the Committee on
Production Guidelines for Book Longevity of the Council
on Library Resources.

Recipes for Roast Bear, Shrimp Stew on the Neuse River,
Claude's Stewed Seafood, Coastal Plain Fish Stew, and
Souse Meat were previously printed in the *North Carolina
Folklore Journal, Volume 52.2.*

Library of Congress Cataloging-in-Publication Data
Edelman, Foy.
Carolina Cooks: favorite main dishes, vegetables, and much
more from the Old North State / Foy Allen Edelman
     p. cm.
Includes index.
ISBN 978-0-9962140-1-8
1. Cooking — American, southern style. 2. Cookbooks

*For all those special people who cook for us,
and who, in the courses of our individual lives,
understand our hungers, feed our bodies and souls,
and nourish our dreams.*

Contents

Potpies & Skillet Dinners 99

Soups & Stews 123

Gravies, Sauces, Marinades, & Salad Dressings 253

Acknowledgments

If the kitchen is the heart of the home, I've had the extraordinary privilege of visiting the great big, generous heart of North Carolina. I will forever be indebted to the cooks across the state who welcomed me and shared their time, recipes, and stories. Thanks to all the people who took time to introduce me to cooks including relatives, friends, neighbors, and members of the North Carolina Agricultural Extension Agency. My deepest thanks to Allison Best Lee, David Teague, and Adam Best Teague for being my gracious hosts in Waynesville while I interviewed cooks in the far western counties. The Blankenship family greeted me on the Qualla Boundary where I stayed in a Cherokee cabin on the mountain behind their home; they introduced me to bean bread and stewed ramps. In Camden County, I helped Sam Staples and his friends prepare for a neighborhood mullet roast by pulling in fish with a net thrown into the Albemarle Sound. Sharon Stroud, currently of Raleigh, is originally from Duplin County. Sharon took me home to visit the family farm and enjoy a lunch of fried pork and rutabagas prepared by her sister-in-law, Billie Stroud. Dawn Scott, an Alamance County native, and Ron Raxter, originally from Transylvania County, kindly invited me to supper where we swapped stories and recipes. I met Brenda Zimmerman, of Salisbury, and Sybil Thomas, of Snow Hill—both became close friends—Sybil sometimes makes my birthday cake. When I visited Wadesboro, Lal and Rachel Johnson prepared a homemade lunch and drove me through Anson County for a tour that included the site of the movie, The Color Purple. Catherine Byrd, originally from Swain County, recounted recipes and stories over a gracious and tasty lunch at her home near Winston-Salem. And when I visited Plymouth in Washington County, I dug into

Mountain Region

Mountain Cooks

AVERY . . . . *Jim & Jennie Vance*

BUNCOMBE . . . . *Jan Collins*

Ruth Graham

Marguerite Hughey

Francis Robinson

BURKE . . . . *Brenda Bowers*

Scheryl Cannon

HAYWOOD . . . . *Nancy Medford Hyatt*

MACON . . . . *Martha Blaine Wood*

CHEROKEE . . . . *Emily Smith*

RUTHERFORD . . . . *Joy Gillespie*

SWAIN . . . . *Dorothy Motsinger*

WILKES . . . . *Retha Durham*

Piedmont Region

Surry   Stokes   Rockingham   Caswell   Person   Vance   Warren

Yadkin   Forsyth   Granville

Alamance   Orange   Durham   Franklin

Guilford

Alexander   Davie

Iredell   Davidson   Randolph   Chatham   Wake

Catawba   Rowan

Lincoln   Lee

Cleveland   Cabarrus   Moore

Gaston   Stanly   Montgomery

Mecklenburg

Union   Anson   Richmond

Piedmont Cooks

ALAMANCE . . . . *Hilda McBane*

CABARRUS. . . . . *Maria Massey Barringer*

Mrs. James G. Dancy

Raymond Frye

Dianne Easley Lambert

Mrs. R. P. York

CASWELL. . . . . *Inez Blackwell*

CATAWBA . . . . *Diana Mauney*

CHATHAM. . . . . *Glennie Beasley*

CLEVELAND . . . . *Terry Self Melton*

DAVIDSON . . . . *Louise Cross*

Jessie Dalton

Ellaree Phillips Everhart

Treva Greer

DAVIE . . . . *Randy Hanes*

DURHAM. . . . . *Jacki Epperson*

Leone Epperson

Tom Epperson, Jr.

FORSYTH. . . . . *Grace Lackey*

Debbie Moose

Rebecca Neff

FRANKLIN . . . . *Cooperative Extension Service*
GRANVILLE . . . . *Sarah A. Elliott*
Marian Moss
GUILFORD . . . . *Mrs. A. W. Byerly*
Helen Cochrane
Moreland Gueth
unknown
Vivian Sullivan
IREDELL . . . . *Jane Lasley*
Rose Speece
Zeb Speece
LEE . . . . *Mildred Rosser Cotton*
MECKLENBURG . . . . . . *Ramona Big Eagle*
Ned Burgess
Susan Cannella
R. H. Stone
MONTGOMERY . . . . . . *Krisan Gregson*
ORANGE . . . . *Liz Bryan*
Mrs. Robert Madry
Dave Mason
Mrs. W. L. Stone
RANDOLPH . . . . *Tom Gray*
Bobbie Jackson
Fred Morgan
Jerry Southard

ROWAN . . . . *Mary Deal*

Jim Graham

Kelaine Zimmerman Haas

Maria Woodson Payne

Brenda Malone Zimmerman

STANLY . . . . *Wanda Brooks*

Jacob Karriker

STOKES . . . . *Elaine Whitaker*

VANCE . . . . *Jennie Corbitt*

Donna Matthews Saad

WAKE . . . . *Will Allen*

Pat Carroll

Margaret Doyle

Rick Hamilton

Sue Kornegay

Kate McKinney Maddelena

Rob Vatz

Inner Coastal Plain Region

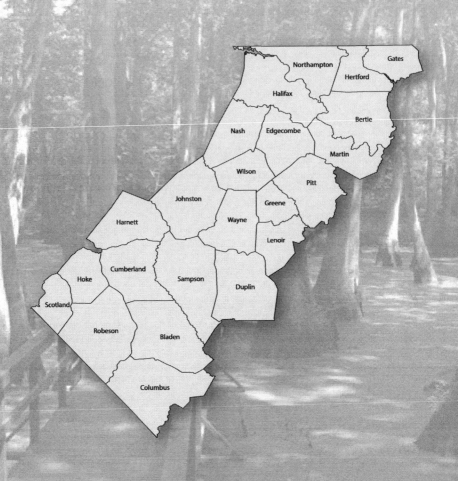

Inner Coastal Plain Cooks

BERTIE. . . . . *Edna Holley*

Katherine Sawyer Ward

BLADEN. . . . . *Margaret Owens*

COLUMBUS. . . . . *Meleah Stanley*

DUPLIN . . . . *Lynda & Bobby Best*

Billie Stroud

EDGECOMBE . . . . *Mary Ella Joyner*

GREENE. . . . . *John Pridgen*

HALIFAX . . . . *Araminta Pierce Blowe*

Marty Pierce Rumley

HARNETT . . . . *Carolyn Goff*

HERTFORD . . . . *Alice Sharpe*

HOKE. . . . . *Polly Barnard*

JOHNSTON . . . . *Brenda Byrd*

Sally Creech

LENOIR . . . . *Reynold Allen*

Sarah Sawyer Allen

Ella Bradshaw

Foy Allen Edelman

Wilbur King

Tidewater Region

Currituck

Camden

Pasquotank

Perquimans

Chowan

Washington

Tyrrell

Dare

Beaufort

Hyde

Jones

Pamlico

Craven

Onslow

Carteret

Pender

New Hanover

Brunswick

Tidewater Cooks

BEAUFORT . . . . *Barbara Everett Roberson*

BRUNSWICK . . . . *Susan Carson*

CAMDEN . . . . *Sam Staples*

CARTERET . . . . *Becky Paul*

Valerie Styron

CRAVEN . . . . *Alice Ward Allen*

Julia Maxwell Allen

DARE . . . . *Fay Kemp Korb*

NEW HANOVER . . . . . . *Brook Dorosko*

ONSLOW . . . . *Nettie King*

PASQUOTANK . . . . *Barbara Newbold Fletcher*

Gladys Umphlett Jennings

Phyllis Looney

Yvonne Mullen

PERQUIMANS . . . . *Buena Walton*

WASHINGTON . . . . *Barbara Hoggard*

Carolina Cooks

"I'm never going to be hungry again.
No, nor any of my folks."

Scarlet O'Hara
Gone with the Wind

Introduction

I opened the front door after a long journey home. My stomach growled as the aromas of roast turkey, cranberries, and pumpkin pie greeted me. Members of my family rose to embrace me in warm hugs and, at the same time, began chattering away. Just like families across the state and country, we'd gathered to celebrate Thanksgiving with our time-honored dinner.

It's comforting to enter a home where a favorite meal is simmering on the stove. For people who love to cook, creating beautiful, healthy dishes is a reward in itself. I find that most people who cook for others are nurturers. They glory in the experience of drawing folks in to sit at their tables and experience the goodness there. "If she doesn't have company coming, she's out looking [for] it," "Mr. Mack" Hudson, of Harnett County, said of his wife Juanita, one of the cooks I met on a trip through North Carolina's 100 counties.

Is it any wonder that home cooking is irresistible? Knowing that we're getting the essential energy we need to fulfill our life demands is primary, but we can get that need met in many places. So why eat at home? First and foremost, it means having the food we like the best prepared our way, through selecting the ingredients we prefer, and putting them together with our particular methods, including herbs and extra twists, to get those satisfying flavors we so enjoy. Also, cooking at home is economical – creating a wholesome and delicious meal often costs less than fast food, so it's certainly a better value. Cooking food in our own kitchens is also a way to connect with nature, our families, and our communities.

North Carolina, where I grew up, is home to an amazing array of agricultural and culinary customs. Rich soils, long growing seasons, and energetic farmers provide us with a cornucopia of local foods from which to choose. In addition, our state has four distinct regions – mountains, piedmont, inner coastal plain, and tidewater – each with its own individual geography, climate, culture, and its own scrumptious local fare. Home-cooked food here is frequently laced with love and spiced with tradition, and you don't even have to be a North Carolinian to join in!

I was suddenly out-placed from my job in 2001. While I looked for another, I started doing something I'd dreamed about for years – visiting cooks in all 100 North Carolina counties and recording their recipes. I had an insatiable appetite for regional victuals, a passion for meeting new people, and a desire to learn more about local history. So I hopped in my Volkswagen New Beetle and happily ate my way across the state. Almost 200 cooks, young and old, from many backgrounds and all parts of the state, shared their favorite recipes. They provided me with the opportunity to connect with my roots and pass on the results to others like you.

As I met folks I asked, "What's your family's favorite dish?" There were many delectable responses to that question: scrumptious pound cakes, ice creams, fruit pies, shortbread cookies, chocolate desserts and candies, and old fashioned butter mints, all presented in the first volume of my discoveries, Sweet Carolina: Favorite Desserts and Candies from the Old North State. However, there were many other answers as well. The recipes mentioned most frequently favored that simple, tasty barnyard bird, the chicken, in a wide array of preparations. Three separate cooks from three different counties give variations on chicken 'n' pastry, perhaps the most often mentioned dish of all the recipes I collected. In addition, chicken and dumplings, chicken salad, chicken pot pies, chicken and rice, fried chicken, and company-coming chicken are included. I marveled that I didn't sprout feathers on my neck and begin to cluck as I tried them all. And though most seafood comes from tidewater counties, it's a statewide favorite. Seafood stew, shrimp Creole, shrimp salad, fried fish, real good oysters, and crab cakes are just a few. When it came to vegetables, cooks fancied locally grown produce: white and sweet potatoes, corn, beans, collards, squash, and asparagus.

While North Carolina is known for its barbecue and ribs, local cuisines vary widely, providing tasters with the opportunity to experience many flavors, styles, and variations on themes. In the mountains I tried Native American bean bread with a side dish of stewed ramps. In the far northeastern counties, I got to taste the local specialty, the boiled dinner, though it took me a while to realize that the dinner was not "bald" as it is often pronounced there, but "boiled"—a mixture of pork, potatoes, and cabbage. Becky Paul, a Cartaret County resident, shared white clam chowder, and from nearby Dare County, Fay Kemp made a dish called picked-up fish, a combination of fresh fried fish with potatoes and onions. Tidewater residents gobble down collard sandwiches made with locally baked light bread. Inhabitants of Scotland County also enjoy collard sandwiches, but like theirs between layers of cornbread. Inner coastal plain counties like Pitt, Lenoir, and Greene are famous for fish stews cooked outside.

I found that generations of creative cooks add their own special ingredients and methods to make individualized versions of traditional dishes to suit those who sit at their own tables. Foods that once fed ravenous farm families who needed hearty meals for their long, hard workdays have been customized for lighter eaters. Meleah Stanley, of Columbus County, makes a heart healthy, low fat version of chicken with pastry. "Her pastry is so delicate you can read a newspaper through it," Meleah's mother, Esther Collier, told me. Kate McKinney Maddalena, of Raleigh, stir-fries sweet potatoes with other vegetables for a tasty and satisfying vegetarian meal. Liz Bryan, of Orange County, sautés her collards in olive oil for a lip smacking "give me more" dish she calls "Chapel Hill collards."

My mouth waters again whenever I remember sampling dishes as I went along. While many of the recipes shared were new to me, most of them are made from ingredients that grow locally and have been enjoyed by North Carolinians for a long, long time.

The great adventure of North Carolina's culinary history began thousands of years ago when the first people migrated from Asia across the Bering Strait and gradually found their way to this special part of the world. Even these early peoples, who became our Native Americans, enjoyed a rich and varied diet in an excellent agricultural environment. They ate corn, sunflower seeds, squash, beans, pecans, black walnuts, cranberries, blueberries, strawberries, maple syrup, prickly pears, grapes, and roots like sassafras. Native Americans hunted and cooked rabbits, turkeys, geese, squirrels, deer, bear, and wild fowl. They enjoyed seafood – clams, oysters, mussels, and fish.

Later arrivals from Europe and Africa joined the Native Americans during the mid-eighteenth century, bringing along foods from around the globe. Grains, pigs, chickens, goats, cattle, apples, and peaches arrived from the Old World. Black-eyed peas, okra, and watermelon came from Africa. Potatoes, tomatoes, and hot peppers came from Central and South America. Since North Carolina is in the middle of the eastern seaboard and has a variety of climates, it was a perfect host for the wonderful variety of people and plants that came here. A great collision of foods and ways of preparing them took place. It was a mighty tasty time in the growth of food traditions, one that still influences our North Carolina cuisine. I think of it as a great, simmering stew pot brimming with ingredients from all over the world.

All these traditions and styles boiled down through the centuries into the local foods we enjoyed when I grew up in Kinston during the 1950s, where cooking styles were straightforward: baking, frying, stewing, boiling, steaming, and broiling. Perhaps this was because fresh, high quality poultry, dairy, beef, pork, vegetables, and fruits were raised locally and didn't need a lot of adaptation to taste good. It may also have been because folks were busy and couldn't always spend a lot of time preparing complex meals.

I grew up in a small, eastern North Carolina town where typical weekday suppers were modest; they included a meat, two or three vegetables or fruits, hot fresh bread, and a dessert. We had smaller portions and simpler foods, like sandwiches and soup, for lunches. We ate weekday suppers and lunches in our kitchen. Sunday dinners often included two or more meats and seafood, with the additions of casseroles, salads, and multiple desserts. They were elaborate meals served in our dining room, where the table had a linen cloth, fine china, silver, and crystal goblets. Everything was prepared at home, and when I visited local farm families, there were many more meats, vegetables, breads, and desserts made ready daily. These were prepared in the morning, eaten for lunch, and warmed over for supper.

On the other side of the state, Debbie Moose in Forsyth County experienced a similar approach to putting food on the table. "We never went out hardly; we'd go out about two or three times a year," Debbie told me, "so we'd have the beef roast, and during the week it was things like vegetable soup or spaghetti, something she [her mother] could cook a lot of, and it was not real expensive, maybe roast chicken, not anything real fancy, and vegetables.

Debbie Moose

My father always had a big vegetable garden in the backyard, because the yard was about an acre in size. That's the one thing I remember that has influenced me. So about half of the yard was his garden; he had corn, butter beans, October beans, and green beans, lettuce, tomatoes, carrots, everything. My mother would freeze or can all that. So we never bought a vegetable except maybe lettuce for a salad in the winter. We could just walk out the backdoor, and pull a tomato off, and then eat it five minutes later, and it was so fresh and so good, and I think that's what I really remember, more than maybe what she did with it, it was how fresh those things were, and how better for us it probably was than if we had been eating something that was canned or frozen with all of whatever they put in there."

My mother was responsible for feeding five people three meals a day for 365 days a year. I calculate that she, like most other women of her generation, prepared 98,550 meals in the course of her three children's eighteen years of living at home. So those folks had lots of cooking experience and really enjoyed swapping recipes. It was about more than just meals, however; it was a beloved lifestyle.

Perhaps an outsider might have looked at our local menus and specialties with no particular interest. After all, that person might come to my hometown in the middle of eastern North Carolina and not see anything notable. The land is flat, so flat that there are miles of highway without a hill or curve. Nor are there any extraordinary landmarks, buildings, or natural wonders. But those of us who grow up in places like Kinston see things differently.

We know that there's a special time of year when the town resembles an artist's palette. White, violet, and purple crocuses, all streaked with delicate yellow lines, peek out first; then camellia blossoms dot huge shrubs with hues of crimson, pink, white, and fuchsia. When forsythia turns from light yellow to golden swirls, local people know that it's spring and that locally grown scallions and strawberries will soon add color and savor to family menus. Before long, the town looks as though it's turned into a Van Gogh painting as banks of azaleas bloom in dazzling shades of red, lilac, white, and translucent lavender; peach, pear, cherry, and quince trees blossom; budding white and pink dogwoods join redbuds in displaying masses of colorful foliage. Like the shad that feel a primal need to race up nearby streams to spawn, the town's fishermen feel the urge to pack their tackle and head east to the Outer Banks where they join thousands of sportsmen throwing out their lines into the Atlantic Ocean to bring in catches that will add welcome tastes to their family's meals. Then the blossoms fade and the fishermen come home and return to their work. The spring show moves out of town to the fruit orchards. The landscapes around town turn into vibrant fields of peaches, corn, tomatoes, potatoes, and soybeans. To the passerby, they're just fields with crops growing in them, and life goes on; but those who look more closely don't miss any of the everyday beauties that make up our lives. Everyone notices when families are expecting babies or losing loved ones, when children graduate from school, homes are improved and gardens planted, when cars are traded, sports won, jobs successfully completed, all events celebrated with food.

And so it is with the simple goodness of home-cooked meals. In our world then, spectacular, multi-course feasts were traditional for Thanksgiving and Christmas. Sunday dinners were solemn and elegant occasions that brought families and friends to beautifully set tables spread with an assortment of dishes. The seasonal menus for everyday lunches and dinners were repetitive and prepared in straightforward ways because they were good and nutritious. Now, with the addition of new foods and ethnic influences, the local diet just keeps getting better and better. Passionate cooks all over North Carolina, whose lifestyles of quiet caring underpin the well- being of local residents, set their kitchen and dining room tables every day. They've inherited, saved, improved, and generously passed on their recipes here.

My small town prided itself not only on its food, but also its collections. Our collections connected us with people, places, and history as much as our diet did. Local men accumulated shotguns, decoys, license plates, and cars. Ladies gathered memorial dishes, quilts, and seashells. Some people collected varieties of flowers; their gardens displayed spectacular jonquils, irises, camellias, or roses. Even children collected dolls, trains, leaves, insects, stamps, a variety of books, local arrowheads, and various wild or exotic animals. While individuals collected many unique items, almost everyone, including men, collected recipes. I brought home recipes from an early age. I've gathered more than 800 North Carolina cookbooks that date back to the nineteenth century. Though the books mostly contain recipes, they also record advice, poetry, quotes, comments, and local histories. I'll be sharing some of the contents of these treasured possessions with you in these pages.

My trip across the state was the most exciting scavenger hunt I could ever imagine. No matter what our differences in geographical location, age, economic and educational background, ethnicity, or politics, it was as though the North Carolinians I met bonded with me when we began speaking what seemed like a Tar Heel food language. Our differences made each trip unique and interesting, and while we shared a statewide language, every community had its own delicious dialect. The recipes are the keepsakes from each excursion, but they're only part of what I ended up bringing back. Each time I ventured out, I met new people who served up a mess of good victuals and introduced me to their localities with pride and openhearted love. Gorgeous and varied landscapes filled with ponds, farms, and magnificent trees welcomed me. Cities seemed to shrink to small towns and towns became neighborhoods as I got to know their people and traditions. Everywhere I went I collected indelible memories of the profuse, yet peaceful, beauty that characterizes our world in North Carolina.

Today the great stew pot of local foods is bubbling over with new ingredients and variations of traditional favorites. I hope you'll share in my culinary journey as you travel through the recipes in this book, get to know the good-natured people who contributed them, and use them to develop your own signature dishes and traditions.

Notes:

- For the most part recipes are presented in a style that lists ingredients at the top and instructions below. Quoted recipes from vintage cookbooks in the introductions are in the words and styles of the cooks being quoted. Some cooks, like Debbie Moose, Barbara Roberson, Billie Stroud, and others describe not just the recipe but how they think about food, its preparation, and presentation. Thus, their recipes are presented in a conversational style.

- As in my extensive North Carolina cookbook collection, some recipes for things like chicken and pastry, vegetable soup, and corn dishes are so popular, imaginative, and diverse that multiple recipes are included.

- Creating main dishes, soups, stews, vegetables, and salads is relatively easy, unlike baking recipes. You don't have to worry about following exact measurements that will lead to failure if not followed precisely. The recipes in this collection are extremely easy to modify and stretch.

- You won't need any specialized kitchen equipment to successfully create these foods. You only need ordinary cookware that includes the typical set of pots and pans, a Dutch oven and/or stockpot, an ovenproof dish, and a frying pan with lid.

- When meat is an ingredient, it is assumed that it is at room temperature.

- The index includes individual entries for vegetarian and "easy" recipes. Recipes that begin with the word "easy" have few ingredients, are quick to make, and are perfect choices for inexperienced cooks. If you're new to cooking, as you explore your kitchen, you'll likely discover that it's full of magic. Cooking at home can be lots of fun and attracts other people, especially when tasty aromas fill the air. I guarantee you that the recipes in this collection are good whenever they're made, and even better when shared. Some recipes have been slightly altered to accommodate modern tastes and health concerns. For example, stuffed peppers can be made with ground turkey as well as ground beef. Easy onion soup can be prepared for vegetarians by making it with vegetarian consommé and a vegetarian bouillon cube.

- One ingredient often used in recipes is red hot pepper sauce. You can use whatever brand you choose, but many of us who grew up here use one called Texas Pete, produced by a company that was started in 1929 by the Sam Garner family of Winston-Salem. With seven children, the family was struggling to survive during the Great Depression. One son, Thad Garner, took his college money and bought a barbecue restaurant that included a secret recipe for barbecue sauce. The restaurant failed in the coming years, but the entire Garner family worked on preparing and canning the barbecue sauce. Sam Garner drove through the back roads of North Carolina selling the sauce. Later, the family developed a piquant sauce called Texas Pete made from hot peppers that grow in Mexico. The family wanted to give the sauce an American name, hence "Texas" in the name, and Pete for one of their sons. In this state folks are very loyal to products that were developed here like Krispy Kreme doughnuts and Bo Jangles chicken. Until I went to college, I never knew there was another "red hot pepper sauce" other than Texas Pete, and I still wonder today what all those other brands are used for.

Main Dishes
& Dressing

For generations, North Carolinians across the state met weekly to share Sunday dinner. It was a social occasion that focused on family rituals and riches. Sunday dinner included all ages, from infants in arms to revered grandparents, gathered around tables laden with the best and most a family had to offer. I can honestly say that I've never had better food in a restaurant than I've eaten around tables hosted by accomplished local cooks comfortable with the hustle and bustle necessary to create the beautiful and tasty meals being served. Sunday dinner wasn't a once-in-awhile event, it was every Sunday and typically included numerous main dishes like fried chicken, roast beef, ham, baked fish, barbecue, and sometimes wild duck or goose all at one meal. Fares throughout the week included many main dishes, though not prepared or served as elaborately. We ate meatloaf, barbecued chicken, fried shrimp and oysters, pork chops and ham, all prepared often and well.

When I traveled as an adult, I was surprised to find out that not everyone in the country or the world ate the variety of protein rich foods that I took for granted. Now I realize how closely North Carolina's agricultural heritage is linked with our culinary history. The intense labor and long hours required to make farms productive also meant that the workforce was hungry, and because of the long growing period and rich soils, that hard work was rewarded with tasty, nutritious, and varied victuals. "Oh, when we grew up, we had lots of food, but most of it was raised at home," Sybil Thomas, now in her nineties and from Snow Hill, told me. "There were six of us: three boys and three girls. We did the typical farming. We raised tobacco and corn. We had lots of tobacco, oodles of tobacco. We put in all week long. We got up early in the morning about 3:30 AM in order to have a barn empty for the day's work. We would work all day until late in the evening. It was just about dark when we finished, and then we had to hang the sticks of tobacco in the barn for curing. By the time we got to the house it was time to eat supper and then bath time.

"We had lots of ham meat with rice and red eye gravy because we raised our own hogs. They boiled the other part. During the winter, when we killed hogs, we had tenderloins for breakfast with rice and gravy. That was wonderful! Daddy would go bird hunting for partridge and he would clean them for cooking. Mama would cook them with gravy, prepare rice, and make the best biscuits in a great long pan, which would carry us through the day. She never cooked supper; we had leftovers. We had cows, plenty of milk, chickens, turkeys, and we had guineas for guinea stew. Guinea is dark meat, which is good, but not as good as chicken; but it's interesting to have."

In Haywood County, Jim and Nancy Hyatt showed me the land her family has farmed for generations. As I was leaving, Jim pointed to the grain corn he grows as feed for the cattle that roam the surrounding pastures. "That's the whole story," he told me. Many of the North Carolinians who shared recipes with me use that beef for making meatloaf, roast beef, beef brisket, country style steak, and delectable hamburgers.

Main dish foods also became important to folks living in towns and cities. Leone Epperson, of Durham, kept a very organized book of handwritten recipes during the 1920s. Here is the introduction to her Meat and Fish chapter:

Meats and fish are of high nutritive value due to their large protein content. Also, when properly prepared, they furnish our bodies with valuable fats, vitamins and minerals and salt.

Today, Raleigh is a large city and the state's capitol. Just after the Revolutionary War, however, it was a small town surrounded by farms and plantations such as one owned by Joel Lane. In 1785, Lane built a plantation house on the outskirts of Raleigh. The house is now known as the Mordecai House and still stands proudly not far from downtown. The well-built house was home to five generations of Lane's descendants. Tobacco, corn, and wheat once grew on the plantation's thousands of acres. Gardens close to the house produced vegetables and herbs used to prepare famous meals with as many as nine courses. "For a dinner of ten or twelve persons, including ourselves," Mrs. Margaret Mordecai Devereux, one of Lane's descendants, wrote in 1933, "there would be a ham at the head, a large roast turkey at the foot, a quarter of boiled mutton, a round of beef a la mode, and a boiled turkey stuffed with oysters. For a larger entertainment a roast pig would be added." You can visit the house today where handsome heirloom dinnerware and intricate sterling silver grace the magnificent, long dining room table as if the Mordecai family is expected for dinner tonight.

Having lots of main dishes had another meaning for some people. My mother, Sarah Sawyer Allen, grew up in Windsor during the Great Depression when times were hard and bragging rights were scarce. "My mother is fatter than your mother," she would declare to her best friend Clara Gatling. At that time, having enough food to become fat was a sign of wealth and status.

Poultry is a favorite in all regions, and not just on farms where killing chickens on Saturday would produce mouth-watering dishes on Sunday. In Carolina Cooking, a book prepared by the Junior Service League in Chapel Hill in 1953, Chapter 8: Poultry, begins with the following introductions given by Mrs. W. L. Sloan:

Chicken is sometimes referred to as the "gospel bird" and these chicken recipes may become your gospel as well as ours. When turkey is the bird in hand, then you need only to look below for complete instructions for preparing turkey, stuffing, and giblet gravy.

SAVORY BREAD STUFFING

12 cups finely broken or diced day-old bread slices
3 cups finely diced celery
2 cups finely chopped onion
1½ tablespoons poultry seasoning
1 tablespoon salt
¼ teaspoon pepper
½ cup melted butter or margarine
½ cup water

Combine dry ingredients in a large bowl. Sprinkle in butter and water
and toss lightly until ingredients are well mixed. Put stuffing by spoon-
fuls in neck opening, using enough to fill the skin. Draw neck skin under
back and sew up with needle and thread. Put remaining stuffing in
body and sew skin. Cross drumsticks, tie securely with a long string, and
fasten to tail. This makes enough for 14-pound turkey.

ROAST TURKEY

Place on its back on rack in dripping pan, rub entire surface with salt,
and spread breast and legs with 3 tablespoons butter, rubbed until
creamy and mixed with 2 tablespoons flour. Moisten a piece of cheese-
cloth large enough to cover turkey and baste with melted butter and
water until the dripping pan has accumulated enough drippings to baste
the turkey from time to time. For basting, use ¼ cup butter, melted in
2/3 cup boiling water. Roast from 3½ to 4 hours at 325°. To test turkey
for doneness, pierce fleshy part of drumstick with 2-tined fork. If done,
fork will go in and out easily. Drumstick also will give readily at leg
joint when moved up and down.

GIBLET GRAVY

Giblets
4 cups cold water
1 onion, sliced
handful celery tops

Combine in a medium-sized saucepan the above ingredients, except the liver. Simmer, covered, about two hours. Add turkey liver and cook 20 minutes longer. Drain stock from giblets; measure; add water to make 4 cups liquid; reserve. Chop giblets and reserve. Remove roasted turkey from pan. Tip pan, pour off fat and reserve, leaving dripping in pan. Blend with drippin's ½ cup reserved fat, ½ cup flour. Stir in 4 cups reserved giblet stock and cook, stirring constantly over low heat until gravy thickens and simmers, 3 minutes. Add giblets and season with salt and pepper to taste.

Much-loved poultry recipes in this chapter include fried, barbecued, roasted, seasoned, and baked, along with a variety of stuffing and dressing recipes that have also been popular for generations.

Pork is another extremely popular meat in North Carolina. Cooks have imaginatively evolved it from basic roast recipes into a vast assortment of satisfying main dishes including tasty variations of barbecue. Phyllis Looney from Pasquotank County shares her mother-in-law's version of the famous boiled dinner, and Inez Blackwell from Caswell County explains how to make souse meat, such a favorite food that one writer waxed poetic when remembering her grandmother's annual ritual to create it.

HOG'S HEAD SOUSE
By Deane Rich Lomax

Hog-killing time at Grandma's house
Would find her making hog's-head souse.
All the hog's head went into that:
Bits of meat and bits of fat,
All the head except the squeal.
Then she stirred in fresh-ground meal;
Salt and spices went in now;
Grandma knew exactly how.
Grandma sliced it gray and cold
And fried it brown in a big black pan.
No wonder grandma held her man!

My vintage North Carolina cookbooks include many ham recipes. I'm not alone in collecting local and antique recipe books; Brenda Zimmerman, of Salisbury, searches them out as well. She invited me several times to visit her in Rowan County when the town held a citywide yard sale at their flea market. We burrowed through stacks of old magazines, newspapers, and books where Brenda found a very worn accounting journal that Maria Woodson Payne, born in Salisbury in 1870, used to record recipes. This recipe is typed in blue on the J. N. Payne and Son stationary that shows it was recorded between 1900 and 1910:

BAKED HAM
Cover ham with cold water and simmer gently long enough to loosen the skin; this will be from two to three hours according to the size of ham. When skinned put in a pan in the oven, pour over it a teacup of vinegar and one of hot water in which dissolve a teaspoonful mustard,

bake slowly two hours basting it often. Then cover the ham all over to the depth of one-inch with coarse brown sugar, press down firmly and do not baste again until the sugar has formed a thick crust, let it remain an hour until it becomes a nice brown. Have a slow oven, take from the oven, drain well when cool. Press by turning a dish on top on which put a weight.

Succulent seafood dishes are diverse and delectable. Nettie King, of Onslow County, tells us how to make crab cakes. Likewise, Sam Staples recounts the story and recipe for finding mullets and roasting them in Camden County; this practice was popular among the Native Americans who once lived in the area. Miss Susie Carson from Southport contributes her mother's recipe for baked flounder, a favorite her family enjoyed during the Great Depression. Brook Dorosko, of Wilmington, makes easy and appetizing clams on the half shell. I grin when I think of Tom Epperson's real good oysters that I sampled in his Durham kitchen. Fay Kemp is from Dare County where her grandmother made picked-up fish from fresh fish and locally-grown potatoes, also included in this chapter.

A collection of main dishes from North Carolina wouldn't be complete unless it included game. Fay told me that her father grew up in Hyde County during the early part of the twentieth century. He and his brother went go out in the fields hunting before school. Whatever they brought back would be on the table that night for supper. My cookbook collection is full of colorful game dishes like this one from 1929:

BAKED O'POSSUM
The o'possum should be dressed in the same way as a pig, and be salted down for at least 24 hours before cooking. Put it to boil in hot water and tie in a nice clean rag a few sprigs of thyme and sage and drop in the water while it is boiling. Let boil until tender and remove from the

water, let drain, slash the skin, sprinkle well with black pepper and a little bit of flour. In the pan in which you bake it you should lay a few twigs from the sassafras bush, which will not spoil but add to the flavor of the meat, and will hold it up out of the grease.

Rick Hamilton worked for the North Carolina Forest Service for many years. While he traveled, he hunted, fished, and cooked with folks across the state. He provides a recipe for succulent duck. Jim and Jennie Vance from Avery County tell the story not only of how to prepare roast bear, but how to hunt for it.

Many main dishes feature vegetables. Bean bread is a special Cherokee favorite. A Piedmont cook provides her version of vegetarian meatloaf made from lentils. We may think that omelets are modern fare, but North Carolina women recorded recipes in eighteenth century cookbooks and these are part of this chapter's bounty. Durham Delicacies are a combination of eggplant and shrimp that'll keep your friends coming back to your table for more. Also, I contribute one of my favorite ways to recreate leftovers by combining them with a baked potato and cheese sauce to quickly make a hearty and attractive meal.

This collection of personal main dish recipes might be considered a culinary autobiography of the state. Some of the dishes, like meatloaf, fried chicken, barbecued ribs, the boiled dinner, and picked-up fish, are so esteemed that they are taste icons. They have understated, but satisfying, flavors. They're simple to make and easy to serve, yet so enduring that they remind me of one of my cooking philosophies: If it's not sentimental, make something else that is. The taste memories are pleasing not just because the foods are good, but also because they connect me with our shared history, the people who enjoyed them with me, and the places where we all live and work.

❧ Beef ❧

Al and Mo's Spicy Meatloaf

ALAN BUNDY, Sampson County

If you think that meatloaf is a tasteless, unrefined dish, maybe trying this one will change your mind. You may want to substitute tomato sauce for the peach salsa and use some extra salsa as sauce. You can add it to the top of the loaf 15 minutes before taking it from the oven. Meatloaf is good served with wild or brown rice. Al and Mo also say that this is a great make-ahead meal that freezes well.

1 pound ground round beef
1 pound ground turkey
1 pound ground pork
*8 ounces mushrooms, sliced and
    cooked*

1 egg
1 cup breadcrumbs
¼ cup parsley, chopped
1 cup peach salsa

PREHEAT OVEN to 350°. You'll need 2 loaf pans, approximately 8- x 4- x 2.5-inches. Combine beef, turkey, pork, and mushrooms until well blended. Add egg, breadcrumbs, parsley, and salsa. Blend until the mixture has a uniform texture. Divide in half, shape each half into a loaf pan. Bake for 1 hour 15 minutes.

Each loaf serves 4 to 6

Easy Meatloaf

BUENA WALTON, Perquimans County

2 pounds ground beef	½ cup milk
1 cup breadcrumbs	1 teaspoon pepper
½ cup chopped onions	¼ cup catsup
1 egg	

PREHEAT OVEN to 350°. Mix all ingredients well. Shape into a loaf. Place in loaf pan approximately 8- x 4- x 2.5-inches. Bake for 45 minutes.

Makes 8 servings

Poyha (Cherokee Meatloaf)

RICK HAMILTON, Wake County

½ cup cornmeal	1 small onion, chopped
½ cup water	1 teaspoon salt
1 tablespoon butter or other fat	2 eggs
1 pound ground beef or venison	
1 medium can (15.25 ounces) whole kernel corn or equivalent fresh corn cut off the cob	

PREHEAT OVEN to 350°. Grease a loaf pan, usually about 8- x 4- x 2.5-inches. Mix cornmeal and water in bowl. Put the fat in a frying pan over medium heat; add the meat, and brown. Reduce the heat and add the onion and corn. Cook for 10 more minutes. Remove from burner. Add the salt and eggs to the cornmeal mixture, and then blend the meat and cornmeal mixtures together. Put in prepared loaf pan. Bake for 35 to 40 minutes.

Serves 4

Beef Barbecue
....

RIXIE STEVENS, Nash County

3 pounds beef roast
2 tablespoons brown sugar
1 tablespoon paprika
1 teaspoon salt
1 teaspoon dry mustard
¼ cup chili powder
2 tablespoons Worcestershire sauce

1/8 teaspoon red hot pepper sauce
* or ½ teaspoon pepper sauce*
½ cup catsup, Rixie prefers Heinz
* brand*
1 cup tomato sauce
¼ cup vinegar
½ cup water

BAKE THE ROAST at 350° for 20 minutes a pound, then remove from oven, and cool. Remove the meat from the roast and chop as you would pork barbecue. Make the sauce by combining the brown sugar, paprika, salt, mustard, and chili powder. When well blended, add the Worcestershire sauce, red hot pepper sauce, catsup, tomato sauce, vinegar, and water. When smooth, put in a saucepan over low heat. When it simmers, add the beef. Continue cooking about 20 minutes.

Serves 8 to 10

Easy Beef Brisket

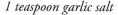

HELEN COCHRANE, Guilford County

1 teaspoon garlic salt

1 teaspoon onion salt

1 teaspoon celery salt

2 tablespoons Worcestershire Sauce

1½ to 2 tablespoons liquid smoke, optional

2 to 3 pounds beef brisket

COMBINE SEASONINGS with the Worcestershire Sauce and liquid smoke; pour over beef. Marinate in refrigerator overnight. When ready to cook, preheat oven to 250°. Remove brisket from marinade and cook in a roasting pan or Dutch oven. Cover brisket with foil; then place lid on roasting pan. Bake for 5 hours. Do not remove lid when cooking.

Serves 8 to 10

Easy Steak Armstrong

HELEN COCHRANE, Guilford County

"This came from Roxy Armstrong's kitchen," Helen told me.

3 cups onions, thinly sliced

3 tablespoons butter or margarine

7 teaspoons paprika, divided

2¼ teaspoons salt

1½ pounds round steak, cubed

about 3 cups water

Sauté onions in butter. Stir in 1½ teaspoons paprika, salt, and meat. Simmer covered for an hour. Then add water and 4½ teaspoons of paprika gradually. Simmer another hour until meat is tender. Sprinkle with remaining paprika when serving.

Serves 6

Beef Roast with Sour Cream Sauce

RICK HAMILTON, Wake County

This is good served over noodles. You can also try it with venison roast.

2 pounds beef roast
¼ cup shortening
1 clove garlic, minced
1 cup celery, diced
½ cup onion, chopped
1 cup carrots, diced
2 cups water
1 teaspoon salt

dash of pepper
1 bay leaf
1 stick (½ cup) butter or margarine, melted
½ cup all-purpose flour
1 cup sour cream
parsley, optional

PREHEAT OVEN to 350°. Remove any fat from the roast and cut into 2-inch cubes. Heat the shortening in a skillet over medium heat, add the meat and garlic, stir until meat is browned. Remove the meat from the skillet to a shallow 2- or 3-quart baking dish, retaining the drippings in the skillet. Add celery, onion, and carrots to the drippings in the skillet; sauté for 2 minutes. Stir in the water, salt, pepper, and bay leaf; pour over the roast. Bake roast for 30 minutes; remove from oven. Drain, reserving broth. Heat butter in a skillet over low heat until melted. Add the flour and stir until smooth. Turn up the burner slightly. Gradually pour in the reserved broth. Cook until thickened, stirring constantly. Blend in the sour cream. When smooth, remove from heat and pour over meat and vegetables. Garnish with parsley.

Serves 8

Country Style Steak

PAT CARROLL, Wake County

Country style steak is one of many recipes where you don't need exact measurements for a delicious outcome. Gather the ingredients, then follow Pat's instructions in the text below.

2 pounds cube steak, tenderized,   *salt to taste*
    cut into 6 pieces   *pepper to taste*
¼ cup vegetable oil   *1 quart water*
½ cup all-purpose flour, divided

"When I fix my country style steak," Pat told me, "I like to make my gravy and put the steak back in it and cover it and just let it simmer. It makes it very, very tender. Mama and Daddy were farmers, and they had eight children so we raised everything in the garden: potatoes, corn, okra, cantaloupe, cabbage, watermelon, squash, tomatoes, cucumbers. We had to feed everybody. It was hard because it was such a large garden. We were sharecroppers and always lived in someone else's house. They would give us land to plant a garden. We might have an acre of watermelons. Daddy sold a lot of watermelons and cantaloupes and cucumbers that we grew. One year he had an acre of cucumbers. We had to pick up cucumbers every morning. We had to move the vines in order to get the cucumbers when they're small, because nobody wanted them when they were large.

"I was the third child from the bottom. Mama taught us how to cook when we were at a really young age. She taught us how to sew at age six. By the time we were seven or eight she had us in the kitchen, and she was teaching us how to cook. When the family was in the field working in tobacco, she would send one or two of us girls back to the house to start cooking lunch for everybody. On a weekday she'd make homemade buttermilk biscuits for supper and fry some fatback and some potatoes, and we usually had some type of beans. On Sunday we had five or six different vegetables and usually fried chicken, because we raised chickens. We took our lunch to school. We took fatback meat and biscuit or a piece of sausage and a biscuit, and if we had leftover fried potatoes from the night before, we had that in a biscuit.

"My mother taught me how to make country style steak. I use good quality cube steak now that's been tenderized. That means that it's been put through a machine and it makes little indentions, holes, in it and that makes it tender. If it hadn't been tenderized, when you fried it, it'd be tough. Mama always used a cast iron skillet. She used lard then because we made it, but I use vegetable oil in a frying pan and get it good and hot. I flour the meat on both sides, put salt and pepper on it, and put it in the hot oil and put a lid on it. Country style steak is pretty thin, so after about ten minutes you flip it over to brown it on both sides. When it's golden brown on both sides, you take it out, and drain it on paper towels. Then, I put a couple of tablespoons of flour into the oil that's left in the pan, turn the heat up, and when it's good and brown I start adding water. Some people use milk but I like water. Gradually I add about a quart of water. I season it with salt and pepper and keep cooking it until it gets to the consistency I want. Then, I add the steak back, cover it, and let it simmer until I'm ready to serve it.

"I'll let it sit there and simmer [perhaps for 30 to 40 minutes]. I have it with cream potatoes or corn or broccoli and cheese, steamed cabbage, and sliced tomatoes."

Serves 4

Tenderloin with Wine Sauce

RICK HAMILTON, Wake County

This is an elegant dish that's easy to make and doesn't leave you with a lot of dirty dishes. Venison T-bone steaks are also good using this recipe. Trim any excess fat from the steaks before cutting them into cubes. You can complete the meal with a fresh salad, roasted potatoes, and hot rolls.

3 tablespoons butter or margarine
4 tenderloin steaks, about 1½
    pounds, cut into ½-inch thick
    cubes
salt and pepper to taste
½ cup dry red wine

1 tablespoon parsley, chopped
1 tablespoon chives, chopped
1 tablespoon quince or currant
    jelly
1/8 teaspoon nutmeg, ground

USE A LARGE skillet over medium heat to melt the butter. Fry the meat 3 or 4 minutes on each side. Sprinkle lightly with salt and pepper; place on warm platter. Combine the wine, parsley, chives, jelly, and nutmeg in the drippings left in the hot pan. Heat until well blended, fragrant, and hot. Spoon over the meat for a gourmet dinner.

Serves 4

Mexican-style Corned Beef and Cabbage

HELEN COCHRANE, Guilford County

"This recipe is from the kitchen of Rebecca Penny," Helen told me.

1 medium cabbage, shredded
1 green pepper, cleaned and
    chopped
1 onion, chopped
½ stick (¼ cup) butter or mar-
    garine
1 can (10.75 ounces) cream of

tomato soup
½ cup water
1 teaspoon chili powder
salt and pepper to taste
1 can (12 ounces) corned beef,
    sliced

PREHEAT OVEN to 350°. Grease a 2-quart baking dish. Sauté cabbage, green pepper, and onion in butter over medium heat for 5 minutes. Pour into prepared dish. Blend tomato soup, water, chili powder, salt, and pepper until smooth, then pour into skillet. Bring to a good boil; remove from heat and pour over vegetables. Put corned beef slices on top. Bake for 20 minutes uncovered.

Serves 4

Easy TV Hamburgers

MARGUERITE HUGHEY, Buncombe County

When this recipe was recorded in 1952, I imagine television was still a novelty in most North Carolina households, but already foods had been developed to be consumed while enjoying the wonders of the black and white screen. 1952 is also the year that TV tray tables were first advertised.

1 pound ground beef
1 cup apples, finely grated, or 1
   cup applesauce

1 tablespoon onion, finely grated
salt and pepper to taste
1 tablespoon Worcestershire Sauce

Combine all ingredients. Shape into 6 patties. Broil in oven 2 or 3 inches from heat or fire up your grill.

Serves 6

Garlic Burgers

···

FOY ALLEN EDELMAN, Lenoir County

When my daughter, Harper, was in high school and college, she and her friends liked burgers cooked on the grill. Fresh Italian style bread was readily available at local stores. One day I decided to introduce the two to each other in this hearty dish. This is a great fan-pleaser during football and basketball seasons.

2 pounds ground round or ground sirloin
2 loaves of Italian bread, uncut
1 tablespoon garlic, minced
1 stick (½ cup) butter or margarine, melted

1 cup mozzarella cheese, grated
1 cup mushrooms, sliced and parboiled, optional
6 slices fresh tomato, optional

PREHEAT OVEN to 375°. Divide ground beef into 6 patties weighing about 6 ounces each; set aside. Slice the 2 loaves of Italian bread the long way, separate the two sides and place them on a counter with insides facing up. Put the garlic and butter into a small saucepan over medium heat. When the garlic begins to brown, remove from heat, and pour evenly over bottom slices of the bread. Sprinkle the cheese over the top slices of bread. Prepare your burgers as you normally cook them. I use a grill, but they can be broiled in the oven or pan-broiled on top of the stove. While the burgers are sizzling, carefully place the 4 long slices of bread in the oven. Watch them closely; when the cheese is melted and the garlic butter is brown and toasty, usually about 8 minutes, turn off the oven. When the burgers are cooked and you're ready to serve, remove bread slices from oven. Drain the mushrooms and spread them evenly over the garlic butter; then add the tomato slices. Place 3 of the burgers on each bottom slice, on top of the mushrooms and tomatoes. Turn the top layers of bread over on top of the hamburgers; slice each loaf into 3 portions. Serve immediately.

Serves 6

Easy Meatballs in the Microwave

KRISAN GREGSON, Montgomery County

"I multiply the recipe to make as many meatballs as I want," Krisan said. "You can freeze raw meatballs until needed. I 'tray freeze' the balls and store them in freezer zip-lock bags. I like to serve meatballs with extra sauce over rice. The sauce is rather tangy as given."

1 pound ground chuck
1 cup minute rice
1 can (10.75 ounces) cream of to-
    mato soup, undiluted, divided
½ cup water

1 egg (or egg substitute)
onion salt to taste
2 tablespoons catsup
1 teaspoon mustard

MIX MEAT, RICE, ½ can of the soup, water, egg, and salt; then form into balls and place into a 1-quart microwave safe dish. For the sauce, blend ½ can soup with catsup and mustard until smooth. Pour the sauce over the meatballs. For each pound of meat, bake 4 minutes, turn and bake 4 more, using meat setting.

Serves 4

Easy Delicious Liver

RUTH GRAHAM, Buncombe County

"This is good served over rice," says Ruth in a note recorded in Favorite Recipes Compiled and Edited by WOMEN'S CIRCLE, Emmanuel Lutheran Church, Asheville, NC, published in 1964.

1 pound beef liver
3 tablespoons butter
1 onion, thinly sliced

1 can (10.75 ounces) cream of mushroom soup, undiluted
salt and pepper to taste

POACH 1 POUND beef liver for 5 minutes, turning once. Remove from pan; slice into very thin strips. Melt butter in skillet, sauté onion and cook until golden. Add liver. Cook 10 minutes longer. Stir in cream of mushroom soup, salt, and pepper.

Serves 4

Ꮿ Poultry & Dressing Ꮿ

Southern Fried Chicken

BRENDA CANNON BOWERS, **Burke County**

Brenda is part of a whole family of good cooks from Valdese. Her mother, Deannie, was famous in Burke County for her fried chicken. It was always the favored dish for Sunday dinner. Brenda's uncle, Sebren, visited after lunch and finished all the rest of the chicken until one day Mr. Cannon had enough of watching the remains of the delicious home cooked dinner disappear. From then on, he hid the leftovers in the oven whenever his brother called on Sunday afternoon. "We used a fresh, whole chicken cut up into legs, breast, thighs, giblets," Brenda told me. "We washed it down the day before it was to be cooked, then soaked the pieces in salt and refrigerated it overnight. The next day we put on old aprons that covered you from shoulders to knees as chicken pops and spatters grease as it fries. This is best when served hot with mashed potatoes, Mr. Cannon's gravy, and homemade biscuits." Brenda's father learned to make gravy while he was a cook in the army. Look in the last chapter, Gravies, Sauces, Marinades, and Salad Dressings, to find his recipe for chicken gravy.

1 frying chicken cut into your favorite pieces
vegetable oil to cover the bottom of a frying pan with lid, Brenda prefers Wesson Oil

1 cup all-purpose flour
salt and pepper to taste
a little water
¼ cup margarine or butter, cut into pats

POUR ABOUT ¾-inch oil in a 2-quart frying pan. Turn burner to medium until the oil is hot but not smoking. Roll each piece of chicken in flour, salt, and pepper. Place chicken pieces carefully in the heated oil. Brown the pieces on either side; this usually takes 7 to 8 minutes per side. Watch it carefully so that it does not burn. Turn down burner to medium low; add a little water to the skillet to keep chicken from sticking. Cover skillet with a lid for 35 minutes; then add 4 or 5 pats of margarine or butter. Cook another 10 to 20 minutes until all pieces are done all the way through. Remove from pan; reserving drippings. Drain well.

Serves 4 to 6

Author's Note:

My mother used a paper or plastic bag to combine the flour, salt, and pepper. Then we shook each piece of chicken in the mixture before placing it in the heated oil. Shaking the chicken gave an even coating of the flour mixture.

To make certain that chicken is completely done, use a meat thermometer pressed into the largest piece of chicken until it reaches 160° F.

Today, sanitation requirements insist that oil and grease be disposed of by placing in a container in the garbage. Never pour oil or grease into the sewer system.

Easy Crispy Chicken

ARAMINTA PIERCE BLOWE, Halifax County

"You can make this dish the day before," says Araminta.

1 cup sour cream	*½ teaspoon salt*
2 tablespoons lemon juice	*1½ cups dry herbed stuffing mix*
2 teaspoons Worcestershire sauce	*8 chicken breast fillets, uncooked*
1 teaspoon paprika	*1 stick (½ cup) butter, melted*
1 teaspoon celery salt	

PREHEAT OVEN to 350°. Grease a 3-quart casserole dish. Blend sour cream, lemon juice, Worcestershire sauce, paprika, and salts together until smooth. Crush stuffing mix into fine crumbs with a rolling pin. Dip each fillet into the sour cream mixture, then into the stuffing crumbs. Roll fillets up and place in casserole dish. Pour melted butter over all. Bake for 45 minutes.

Serves 8

Barbecue Chicken Beaverdam Style

RAYMOND FRYE AND J. D. HOWARD, Cabarrus County

This recipe is recorded in a 1948 cookbook entitled The Daily Independent Cook Book 1948: A Collection of Favorite Recipes Tested and Proved in Kannapolis Area Kitchens by Some of North Carolina's Best Cooks. Beaverdam, North Carolina, however, is in Buncombe County. There's no note indicating from where Misters Frye and Howard got this recipe, but it sounds like a family favorite to me.

The recipe is in three parts: boiling the chicken, making the sauce, and then combining the chicken with the sauce. You can make the sauce while the chicken cooks.

1 large roasting or frying chicken
½ cup catsup
1 cup vinegar
½ small onion, chopped, or ½
* teaspoon garlic, minced*
1 teaspoon dry mustard
1 teaspoon Worcestershire Sauce

1 teaspoon salt
½ teaspoon red hot pepper sauce
¼ teaspoon ground clove
vegetable spray or ½ stick (¼
* cup) butter, softened to room*
* temperature*

BOIL CHICKEN, whole, until tender.

To make the sauce, combine catsup, vinegar, onion or garlic, mustard, Worcestershire sauce, salt, red hot pepper sauce, and clove in a saucepan. Simmer for 10 to 20 minutes over medium heat. Remove saucepan from heat.

PREHEAT OVEN to 325°. Grease a roasting pan with vegetable spray or butter. When the chicken is done and drained, split it in half lengthwise. Place it in the prepared roasting pan. Pour the sauce over the chicken halves evenly. Bake for 55 minutes or until golden brown, basting the meat with the sauce every ten minutes.

Serves 4 to 6

Easy Chicken Breast Supreme

SALLY CREECH, Johnston County

1 package (3 ounces) chipped beef	*1 can (10.75 ounces) cream of*
4 boneless, skinless chicken breasts	*mushroom soup*
4 slices bacon	*1 cup sour cream*

PREHEAT OVEN to 250°. Separate pieces of beef and spread on bottom of a two-quart baking dish. Roll each chicken breast with a piece of bacon. Place on top of chipped beef. Combine soup and sour cream. When blended, spread over chicken. Bake uncovered for 3 hours.

Serves 4

Easy Company's Coming Chicken and Shrimp

BROOK DOROSKO, New Hanover County

"If you find out about an hour before they arrive that company's coming for dinner, use this recipe," Brook told me. "I keep chicken and shrimp frozen for times like this. You may think you have to have white wine with chicken, but red is good too. You want to experiment with types of tomato sauce. Some have Mexican flavors; others have Italian. They'll all work, but you want to find the one that delivers just the right flavors for you. When you add the shrimp, it soaks up the juices and flavors. Serve this over rice or noodles. It doesn't get any easier or better than this."

2 tablespoons butter

4 boneless, skinless chicken breasts
    cut into 1-inch square pieces

1 small onion, chopped

¾ teaspoon garlic, minced

salt and pepper to taste

½ cup wine

1 teaspoon fresh basil, chopped

1 jar (24 ounces) tomato sauce

1 pound raw shrimp, shelled and
    deveined

1 tablespoon fresh parsley, chopped

MELT THE BUTTER in a Dutch oven over medium heat. Pour in the
chicken, onions, and garlic. Stir the mixture until it browns a little.
Season with salt and pepper; then pour in the wine and sprinkle with
basil. Keep stirring while you pour in the tomato sauce. Turn the burner
down so that the mixture will simmer for 15 minutes without burning.
Then add the shrimp and parsley. Stir about 3 minutes, or until the
shrimp is pink but not hard. Serve immediately.

Serves 4 to 6

Debbie Moose's Mama's Chicken and Rice

DEBBIE MOOSE, Forsyth County

Debbie Moose is a much-loved North Carolina food writer. She is a former
food editor at the News & Observer and the author of many cookbooks
including my favorite, Deviled Eggs: 50 Recipes from Simple to Sassy.

"I was born in Charlotte," Debbie told me, "but I was only there long
enough to get born. My father, Everette Pinkney Moose, soon got a job
in Winston-Salem. Technically, I grew up in the city limits, but at first it
was really more like being out in the country because my parents' house

was in a development. It was on one side of the two-lane blacktop, and it was all the little 1950s ranch houses and split-levels the way they used to build them back then with teeny little houses on great big lots, because I guess building was more expensive than land back then. Right across the blacktop was a Black Angus cattle farm that was huge. In fact, I think the land where the development was put had originally belonged to the farm. They gave land for the church that was built about half a mile down the road too. I remember going with my parents up to the barn to have church before the church was built, and we'd sit on bales of hay and have church in the barn. The farm was rolling fields and black cows in green fields. It was really pretty. Then they got a white Brahma bull at one point so then the cows started turning brown and spotted. The people who owned the farm didn't mind if people walked around there. They had a farm pond, and they had horses. It was almost like having a park, because they were very open to people coming up there and walking around, and we'd ride our bikes. Sometimes one of the cows would get out, and we'd find it in our front yard.

"My mother, Juanita Emma Shaw was from Statesville in Iredell County; she stayed home. My father came home for lunch, because he only worked about ten minutes away, and there was no place to eat around there. He didn't read a lot of books, but he would read every word of the newspaper. We had a morning and an evening newspaper then. He'd start the morning paper before he went to work and finish it when he came home at lunchtime. When he got home at night, he'd read the evening paper. For lunch she didn't really do too much; for weekday lunch it was usually sandwiches like in the summertime, good old tomato sandwiches with tomatoes out of the garden. The big meal was in the evening. Cooking was not a big activity for my mother. Bless her heart. She didn't really enjoy it. We used to joke that there were five things that she would cook, and you'd see them on the same days of the week. For people who didn't have parents who grew up during the Depression, none of us ever realized what that was like, and I think there was always this feeling among those people that there might not be any more tomorrow. She wasn't one to waste food or spend a lot of money on food. Usually she would make maybe a beef roast on Sunday. And she believed in cooking things very thoroughly. I was in college before I realized meat came in any other color other than black. She got mad when she came here to visit because she complained I served her raw food.

"On Saturday nights we'd often have steaks with a baked potato. One thing that I still cook of hers that I like a lot is chicken and rice. It's nothing fancy, but it just tastes good on a cold day. There's really not a recipe for it. It kind of depends on how much you want to make. You have chicken parts or a chicken cut up into parts. Sometimes I just buy the parts I like, like thighs or breasts. In a big baking pan, like a 9-x13-inch pan, or sometimes I use two pans, if I want to make enough for leftovers. Melt a couple of tablespoons of butter in the bottom of the pan. I often do that by sticking it in the oven while the oven is preheating to 375°. When the butter can just be melted, you put in your chicken parts and turn them over to coat them with butter. Don't fill the pan too full so you'll have room for the rice. Around the pieces pour about a cup, cup and a half of rice, again it depends on how big your pan is, and it needs to be white rice. I tried brown once and it didn't get cooked. And it's also important not to get any of the rice on top of the chicken, because that's not going to cook, and it will be all crunchy and icky. That's why you have to pour it in around the chicken. Then she used to use a chicken bouillon cube, and I use canned chicken broth instead, because I think that tastes better, it's not as salty, and because I don't use bouillon cubes. She used them for everything. So pour chicken broth around that and then some water until it's just full of water. You want enough water there to cook that rice. I usually sprinkle a little salt and pepper and maybe a little garlic powder, she didn't do that but I do, or onion powder and then maybe a little paprika to give it some color. And then seal that up by putting a lid on it or some foil and seal it up. Put that in the oven. You want to leave that lid on it so the rice can cook. But after about maybe 20 minutes you want to peak at it to see if the water is cooking away. If the water is cooking away and it's drying out, you may need to add some more chicken broth or water to get the rice cooked. It takes anywhere from an hour to an hour and fifteen minutes, depending on how much you have in the pan, until the chicken's cooked through. And usually for the last ten or fifteen minutes before it's done I take the lid off so the chicken can brown a little bit. And that's really all there is to it. It's just flavorful and good and simple. It's comfort food."

2 tablespoons butter

1 baking chicken cut into parts, or your favorite equivalent chicken parts

1½ cups white rice

2 cans (14.5 ounces each) chicken

broth

salt and pepper, to taste

garlic powder, to taste, optional

onion powder, to taste, optional

paprika, for garnish, optional

PREHEAT OVEN to 375°. Put the butter in the bottom of a 9- x 13-inch baking pan, then place the pan in the oven until the butter is melted. Rub each piece of chicken into the butter, then turn it over, and arrange the pieces in a single layer in the pan. Pour the rice between the chicken pieces, being careful not to get grains on the chicken itself. Slowly pour in the chicken broth. Season to taste with salt, pepper, garlic, and onion powders. Sprinkle chicken with paprika. Cover the chicken tightly with foil. Put in oven. Check the liquid level after 20 minutes; if it's cooking away, you need to add water. Replace the foil; continue cooking for 40 more minutes, then remove the foil. Cook another 20 or so minutes, until chicken is cooked all the way through, and the rice is soft.

Serves 6

Stuffed Peppers

GRACE LACKEY, Forsyth County

This recipe comes from Bethabara Cook Book published sometime before 1963. Original instructions include using a muffin tin to cook the peppers. You can do this, though today our green peppers are typically larger than the ones that we grew when I was young. Thus, they may not fit into the spaces that are standard in muffin pans today.

8 green peppers	*2 cups tomatoes, chopped*
2 tablespoons shortening or grease	*1½ cups corn*
1 small onion, chopped	*salt and pepper*
1 pound ground turkey or beef	*buttered crumbs*

PREHEAT OVEN to 350°. Cut tops and remove seeds from peppers leaving the bottoms whole. Cook the peppers in boiling water for 5 minutes. Invert to drain. Melt shortening or grease over medium heat in skillet. Brown onions and beef; add tomatoes, corn, and season to taste. Remove from heat. Cool slightly, then stuff the onion and meat mixture into the peppers. Pour about ¼ cup boiling water into the bottom of an ovenproof dish or pan approximately 8¼ inches square. Arrange the stuffed peppers in the dish; bake approximately 1 hour.

Serves 8

Saffron Rice with Chicken Livers and Mushrooms

VIVIAN C. SULLIVAN, Guilford County

My brother, Will Allen, and I attended North Carolina State University at the same time during the 1960s. The night of my 19th birthday in 1969, Will took me to the restaurant in Mission Valley Inn, on Western Boulevard in Raleigh, then the meeting place of the Wolfpack Club. The restaurant had a well-dressed African-American chef who made this dish for our dinner. Where I come from we call this succulent blend of tastes and textures "bodacious." I looked for the recipe for years until I found it in The Quaker Cookbook, Quaker Recipes Collected by Members of the Woman's Auxiliary of High Point Friends Meeting published in Greensboro in 1954. It was well worth the years of searching.

2 tablespoons olive oil	1 ½ cups chicken broth
1 medium onion, finely chopped	1 stick (½ cup) butter
½ clove garlic	1 pound chicken livers
1 cup uncooked rice	1 cup fresh mushroom, cleaned
¼ teaspoon saffron	and chopped
½ teaspoon salt	

PUT OLIVE OIL in top of double boiler set over a burner on low heat. Gently fry onion and garlic. When tender, discard garlic; pour in cup of rice, saffron, and salt. Stir well and add just enough chicken broth to cover. Cook uncovered in double boiler until tender, adding more broth as needed. Stir gently with wooden fork to keep from breaking grains. While the rice cooks, melt the butter in a frying pan over medium heat. When completely melted, stir in the livers, and sauté until cooked all the way through. Stir in the mushrooms until well blended. Turn heat to low until rice mixture is cooked. When rice is tender, turn into a shallow pan and dry in a warm – not hot – oven. Rice should be quite dry. Arrange rice in circle on platter and fill the center with chicken livers and mushrooms. Divine!

Serves 4

Rob's Coca Cola Turkey
. . . .

ROB VATZ, Wake County

"Because of where he grew up," Debbie Moose told me, "my husband, Rob Vatz, liked to eat a lot of old southern food. Now the 'Coca Cola Turkey,' I can tell you the story as good as he could. When I got married my husband, Rob, kept telling me about this Coca Cola marinated turkey that his Aunt Ida would make in Kinston near where he grew up. Back when I was first here, I had to work at Thanksgiving. I was on the copy desk at the Raleigh Times. Somebody's got to work, and I said to him, 'If you want Thanksgiving dinner, you're going to have to cook it, because I'm working.' And Rob said he'd do the Coca Cola turkey. It was the most amazing thing. It looked like one of those magazine cover turkeys when it came out this brown color. The breast meat was so moist; you know how the breast meat sometimes gets so dry. I was a convert to the Coca Cola turkey after that.

"His aunt Ida was one of those cooks who never wrote anything down. The way he had to get the recipe was that he and his cousin had to go over there and watch her make it and literally grab her hand when she got ready to throw something in and stop and measure it.

"It's basically Coca Cola and it has to be regular Coke, not diet, and orange juice. It's not quite equal portions of each. And before you pour that one, his Aunt Ida used to use seasoned salt, but Rob never has used that. He used paprika and salt and pepper and a crushed bay leaf on it. You pour the Coca Cola and orange juice over it. Obviously you can't get enough to fully submerge the turkey. You marinate it overnight, spoon it over that mixture over it. Then drain that off. When you get ready to roast it, you put an apple inside the turkey. He cuts up carrots, onions, and celery, and puts that in the bottom of the roasting pan with a little bit of water. So it sort of roasts, and it sort of steams. I guess that's what makes it nice and brown, the sugar in the Coke and the orange juice. You don't taste it, even if you eat a piece of the skin, but it just comes out beautiful. Nobody who's ever tried it has ever gone back. I know people who do that and then deep-fry it. There's such a tradition in the South of cooking with soft drinks. There really is."

1 roasting turkey, thawed to room temperature
64 ounces regular Coca Cola
2 cups orange juice
paprika, salt, and pepper to taste
1 crushed bay leaf
1 apple
2 carrots, peeled
1 large onion, peeled and quartered
2 stalks celery, washed

The day before you plan to cook your turkey, place it in a turkey roaster or Dutch oven. Pour the Coca Cola and orange juice over it. Season to taste. Spoon the mixture over the turkey, cover, and refrigerate. Periodically remove the turkey and baste with the Coca Cola/orange juice mixture. When ready to cook, preheat the oven to 325°. Drain off the marinade. Cut up the apple and place inside the turkey cavity. Arrange the vegetables around the turkey and add enough water to cover the bottom of the roasting pan. Bake until the internal meat temperature is 165°, usually about 20 minutes per pound. Remove and cool before slicing.

A whole turkey yields about 2.8 servings per pound according to the National Turkey Federation.

Smoked Turkey

DAVE MASON, Orange County

Dave Mason learned to cook just after his marriage in 1965. He grew up working in a variety of restaurants in New York and North Carolina, including the Ranch House in Chapel Hill. "I'm a perfectionist about my cooking," he told me. He's created sauces for steaks, and is famous among his friends for his turkey recipes. You'll need a dome smoker to make this fabulous turkey. I've also used the technique to smoke chicken.

a fresh turkey　　　　　　　　*a dome smoker*
Kosher salt　　　　　　　　　*at least 10 pounds of charcoal*
3 ounces pickling spice

SALT THE TURKEY thoroughly inside and out the day before you want to cook it. Refrigerate for 24 hours. Remove from refrigerator and rinse five or six times. The dome smoker has three levels. The bottom pan will contain charcoal. The middle pan will be filled with water. The turkey will be placed in a pan uncovered on the rack at the top of the smoker. Water and pickling spice will be placed in the bottom of the pan containing the turkey. Start your fire in the bottom pan using about 5 pounds of charcoal. Light it and get it good and hot until it is gray in color. Place 4 or 5 chunks of wet hickory wood on the sides of the charcoal. Let the fire sit until it creates a lot of smoke. Place water in the pan directly over the charcoal. Put the turkey in the pan with the pickling spice dissolved in water on the rack at the top of the smoker. Leave the turkey in the smoker for approximately 8 hours. The fire will die out after 4 hours. Rekindle the charcoal as you did to begin with and let cook another 4 hours.

A whole turkey yields about 2.8 servings per pound according to the National Turkey Federation

Easy Southern Dressing

RICK HAMILTON, Wake County

"Bread should be 2 or 3 days old, but not stale enough to be dry," says Rick.

Thanksgiving is my favorite holiday. I always use poultry seasoning in the traditional turkey dinner that is my all-time favorite meal to prepare. All it takes is one tiny whiff of this pungent combination of herbs and spices to bring back sixty years of happy Thanksgiving memories – some were remarkable feasts celebrated at grand tables with beautifully-outfitted companions, others were simple meals with a few close, casually-dressed friends. But all those memories flow as freely through my consciousness as gravy does on a warm piece of turkey when I inhale the mixture of salt, sage, thyme, marjoram, rosemary, nutmeg, and black pepper. Though it's especially good with poultry, Rick likes this seasoning in the dressing that he sometimes eats with baked raccoon.

6 slices white bread
1/3 cup yellow corn meal
½ cup onions, finely chopped
2 tablespoons parsley, finely
*   chopped*
dash of pepper

1 teaspoon poultry seasoning or
*   sage*
1 cup coon (raccoon) or chicken
*   broth*
1 cup milk

TEAR BREAD into coarse crumbs; drop into a mixing bowl with the corn meal, onions, parsley, pepper, and sage. Blend thoroughly before stirring in the broth and milk.

Serves 8, enough for 4 to 5 pounds of fowl or 2 to 3 pounds of baked raccoon

Cornbread Dressing

WILL ALLEN, Wake County

When my brother, Will Allen, moved to Raleigh to attend college during the 1960s, he supplemented his income by working at Baxley's, a local family-type restaurant located on Hillsborough Street across from the campus. There Will learned to make this traditional favorite.

½ cup celery, chopped
1 cup onion, chopped
¼ cup green pepper, chopped
½ cup shortening
½ cup white bread, torn into
*   small pieces*

4 cups corn bread, torn into small
*   pieces*
2 cups chicken broth
salt and pepper, to taste

PREHEAT OVEN to 375°. Grease a 12- x 18-inch baking pan. Combine all ingredients; then pour into baking pan and smooth out. Bake for 45 to 60 minutes or until brown.

Serves 8

ℰꙨ Pork ℰꙨ

Baked Ham in a Paper Bag

JULIA MAXWELL ALLEN, **Craven County**

"I majored in home economics at Salem College in Winston-Salem," my Aunt Julia told me. "This is one of my favorite recipes to have when my family comes."

a ham, uncooked	*2 teaspoons ground cloves*
2 cups brown sugar	*4 cups orange juice*

PREHEAT OVEN to 325°. Use a large brown paper grocery bag to wrap around your ham, then place it in a roasting pan. If the ham is 12 pounds or under, bake it in the bag for 22 minutes per pound. If the ham is over 12 pounds, cook it for 18 minutes per pound. Take it out of the oven about 45 minutes before it's done. Take it out of paper bag, but leave the ham in the roasting pan. Remove skin. Combine the brown sugar, cloves, and orange juice. Slice the top so that the brown sugar mixture can be packed down into the meat. Pat the mixture down into the slices. Put the pan back into oven (without paper bag) until a meat thermometer registers 150° internally. Be sure that the meat thermometer is placed in the thickest part of the meat not near the bone.

Yields 2 to 3 servings per pound according to the North Carolina Pork Council

Easy Ham and Asparagus Quiche

MARGUERITE HUGHEY, Buncombe County

You can omit the ham and add a cup of chopped mushrooms or another cup of asparagus for a vegetarian quiche.

1 pie crust
1 cup cooked ham cut into small pieces, ¼-inch if you can
1 cup asparagus, cooked
1 cup Swiss cheese, grated
3 eggs, beaten
1 cup milk
salt and pepper, dash of each

PREHEAT OVEN to 350°. Line a pie plate with the piecrust. Sprinkle ham evenly in bottom. Arrange asparagus over ham. Sprinkle cheese evenly over all. Combine eggs, milk, salt, and pepper until smooth. Pour over ham, asparagus, and cheese. Bake 30 to 40 minutes until set.

Serves 6

Sauerkraut Dumplings

DIANA POWELL MAUNEY, **Catawba County**

Diana is the descendent of both Catawba Native Americans and German immigrants. Her family enjoyed this recipe frequently when she grew up in Newton-Conover.

1 small pork roast
2 pounds of sauerkraut
salt and pepper, to taste

red pepper, to taste
10 uncooked biscuits homemade
or from a can

COOK PORK on top of stove in a Dutch oven, using enough water to cover the roast. Boil until the internal temperature is 145°; then remove from heat and drain the roast, reserving the water it cooked in. Let it cool, debone the meat and remove the fat, then put meat back in water. Add kraut, salt and pepper to taste, and red pepper to taste. Bring back to a boil. Add the biscuits; you may drop in whole or roll out and cut into strip dumplings. Cover and reduce heat. Simmer for about 25 to 30 minutes. Stir occasionally.

Serves 6 to 8

Piedmont Barbecue

MARGUERITE HUGHEY, Buncombe County

1½ pounds beef

1½ pounds pork

1 large onion, chopped

1 cup catsup

3 to 4 tablespoons vinegar

1 to 2 tablespoons dry mustard

salt and pepper, to taste

red hot pepper sauce, to taste

PRESSURE COOK the meats together for 45 minutes. Tear the meat into pieces and transfer it to a Dutch oven, adding the onion. Combine the catsup, vinegar, mustard, salt, pepper, and hot sauce. Pour over the meat and onion. Simmer for one hour.

Makes 3 pounds

Easy Barbecued Frankfurters

MARGUERITE HUGHEY, Buncombe County

1 teaspoon onion flakes or fresh

onion, chopped

1 teaspoon dry mustard

1 cup tomato juice

1 tablespoon sugar

¼ cup vinegar

dash of salt and pepper

12 frankfurters, slit lengthwise

PREHEAT BROILER. Combine onion, mustard, tomato juice, sugar, vinegar, salt, and pepper. Heat until slightly thickened. Place frankfurters under broiler; spread with half the sauce. Broil until brown. Turn and spread with remaining sauce and brown.

Makes 4 servings

Eastern Style
North Carolina Barbecue

BOBBY BEST, Duplin County

"I'm from Warsaw in Duplin County," Bobby told me. "That's the country. I'm from the country; we always farmed. Well I remember we used to barbecue pigs on the farm, pigs that we had grown. We would take them [to an abattoir] and have them slaughtered, we would bring them back and barbecue them on the farm. We would dig a small pit down in the sand, and put rows of cinder blocks down about four feet apart, and then we would get hardwood out of the woods, oak trees, and we would start coals in that pit. Once we had the pit started with coals, we would lay some pipes on top of the cinder blocks, and we would lay the pig on top of the pipes. We would put it what we called 'face down' for about an hour. Then we would turn it over and cook it for several more hours and keep feeding more and more coals underneath it until we got it to the temperature we wanted. We didn't cover it.

"Other people around did other things. Back a long time ago some people around here even put the pig down into the pit and covered it and the coals with dirt. What they would do is like what we do which is get oak trees, and a lot of coals, and put it down in that pit, and lay tin on top of those coals, and then lay the pig on top of the tin itself. Then they would put tin over the top of the pig and cover it with sand completely. This would take several hours also. It's amazing that you could put coals in this thing one time, and it would completely roast the pig, but it would.

"We would start ours when we started our usual daily routine," Bobby continued. "If it took six, seven, or eight hours, in the afternoon is when we would usually have the pig eating part of the barbecue. We'd invite some neighbors or friends over. I remember Daddy would pull a rib off to see if he thought everything was correct or not, but we never had a meat thermometer or anything. He took hold of the ham itself, and if that bone began to break and come away from the ham, he knew it was nearly done. When it was almost done, we would begin putting vinegar and hot peppers on it for it to cook a little bit longer, just a little bit longer. Then we would take it off and chop it up. We always had what we called a wash pot, but it was made out of wood. That's where we always chopped the barbecue up in it. We'd chop it up and keep tasting it, and adding more hot pepper to it until we got it to the place where we wanted it as far as taste is concerned.

"Now when we have one, we have a barn where we have a 500 gallon drum that we cut in half, and we had a grate put across the top of it, and we mounted gas burners under it, so we do all of it by gas now. [It's] nothing like it used to be when we did it by wood. But everything else is pretty much the same as far as the vinegar and peppers and chopping and mixing. That's pretty much like it's always been.

"Usually you've invited people who are around when the pig is ready and, of course, we have slaw and potato salad and some cornbread. A pig pickin' is usually a big deal, a neighborly thing, and family thing, and some of our kin people come. Most of the time we eat outside under a barn or something. People get a plate and get what they want, and we always have a big jug of iced tea."

Barbecued Ribs

MARY JOYNER, Sampson County

This same recipe is just as good for beef ribs. It's from Something Old – Something New, authored by the Woman's Club of Clinton in 1975.

3 to 4 pounds pork ribs
½ cup all-purpose flour
1½ cups barbecue sauce
½ cup green pepper, chopped

½ cup onion, finely diced
½ cup celery, diced
salt and pepper, to taste
dash of oregano

PREHEAT OVEN to 300°. Trim the ribs of excessive fat and cut into individual serving pieces. Combine flour with barbecue sauce, green pepper, onion, celery, and seasonings. Place ribs in a baking pan approximately 2½-inches deep. Pour the sauce over the ribs. Cover the pan with aluminum foil. Pierce the foil a half dozen times with a sharp knife. Bake for 2 to 2½ hours.

Serves 4 to 6

Souse Meat

INEZ ELIZABETH GRAVES BLACKWELL, Caswell County

Without the assistance of the North Carolina County Extension Agents for Family and Consumer Education, this collection of recipes and stories would not be possible. Donna Pointer was the Caswell County Extension Agent when I met Inez Blackwell initially. Even if Mrs. Pointer had not introduced me to Mrs. Blackwell, almost anyone in Yanceyville could have;

they all know her. Mrs. Blackwell has written a column called "Yanceyville News" in the local weekly newspaper, the Caswell Messenger, for over thirty seven years. She's covered topics from watermelon to sidewalks to respect for the elderly to "whatever crosses my mind," she says.

I met with Mrs. Pointer and Mrs. Blackwell to talk about culinary traditions in Caswell County. Mrs. Pointer moved to Yanceyville thirty eight years ago and remembers going to meetings where the most popular dessert was plain white pound cake served with sweet pickles. Mrs. Blackwell has always lived in Caswell County and says the most popular meal consists of turnip greens, corn bread fritters, and chitterlings. The favorite desserts are apple pecan cake, and sweet potato and coconut pies. If you have a hankering for authentic ashcakes or Brunswick stew prepared over an outdoor fire, you might want to put on your square dancing shoes and drive toward the Virginia border the last weekend in September when Yanceyville holds the Annual Brightleaf Hoedown in the town square.

"(My name is) Inez Elizabeth Graves Blackwell and my nickname, Sis. Story behind my name. Ma and Fanny wanted her name to be Inez. So when my mama had me, she asked my [grand]mother to name me Inez. She did and she added her name, Elizabeth. I was born in Caswell County, Yanceyville, North Carolina, December 13, 1930. My parents, William Barnard Graves, Carrie Elizabeth Slade Graves. When I was born I had six fingers on my left hand and my grandmother, Golden Slade, tied a string around it, let it stay on until the finger came off. I was raised by my grandparents, Willy and Golden Slade. They had twelve of their own and raised my brother, Walter, and I. It was years before I knew that I wasn't one of their own. Mama and Papa explained to me that my mama was Carrie that lived in Durham. From that day on, I was afraid of her because I thought she would take me from Mama and Papa.

Grandmother took me to live with her when I was very small.
She said to me, "Remember you can stay short or you can grow tall.
You will find out in life you are going to face many trials and lots of
strife,
But always keep God by your side.
Let him be your leader and your guide.
Try to do your best in school.
Never forget the golden rule.
You know I have tried to raise you up in the right way,
Because you'll be grown and on your own one day.
But don't ever forget to kneel down and pray.
Then the Lord will help you on your way.
Try to help someone as I did you.
God will tell you what to do.
Treat your fellow man as your friend.
God will be with you until the end.
Hold you head high and walk with pride,
And God will walk right by your side.
Continue to be good, remember to stand tall
Keep God in mind, you will never fall.
These are memories I will never forget and love the best,
Now that my dear grandmother, mother, has gone home to rest.
Golden Phillips Slade Bow

"They moved around a lot because they were sharecroppers, farm workers; so if someone offered Papa more money and a better house, we moved. That is why I always said as a child, when I grew up I was going to have my own home and, thank God, I have my own home. They raised pigs, chickens, had cows. I had a pig until hog killing time. I never did like to be around when the hog killing, because I always had to cry when they kilt my pig.

"We had chores in the morning before we went to school and at night, bringing in wood, going to the spring for water, cleaning the lamp every day, helped to clean the house, helped wash the clothes in tin tubs, bringing water to wash the clothes with, taking care of the younger children, also picked fruits and berries, and worked in the tobac. You name it, we did it. So we played hopscotch, jump rope, circle games, rolling tides, baseball with homemade balls, tobacco thread, playing with corn shucks dolls, making our own playhouse, and throwing snow balls, and so forth.

"We grew everything and Mama canned and preserved everything. Mama did all of the cooking until Fanny and those got old enough to start cooking, and then she started working outside the home; so she left Fanny and Golden and the girls there to do the cooking at home. One house lady would try to get her from the other house lady. 'Come work for me, come work for me.' She had a plenty of jobs, because she was a real good cook. My daddy loved pork chops, and he loved cheese and eggs, and gravy, hot biscuits, and ham or some fatback meat nearbout every Sunday.

"This is a treat that I always made at Christmas, and I usually give some to some friends. And when we would kill hogs, I would always go somewhere and get the hog head, the pig feet, and the pigtails, came home, and cleaned them, and soaked them in salt water overnight. The next day I would cook them, take all the meat off them, and set it aside, and let it get cold, so I could work with it with my hands and get all of the bones out of it, then I would season it with salt and pepper and then have me something like a cake pan, press it down real hard. Put it in the refrigerator until it chill. After it chill real good, you take your knife, and it will cut real pretty. And you put it in some vinegar and then you could serve it. But you don't have to put it in vinegar, 'cause you can make sandwiches out of it, or you can eat it with crackers, but I usually like to put it in the vinegar, 'cause I like to eat it with my beans, and you can eat it with turnip greens, cabbage, just mostly anything. It's just a good meat. I always make some at Christmastime, don't seem right if I don't have some."

Amelia Turner's Boiled Dinner

PHYLLIS LOONEY, Pasquotank County

"My grandmother would serve rutabagas and turnips with her boiled dinner," Phyllis told me. "She would mash boiled vegetables together and add butter, salt, and pepper. Every Saturday lunch my grandmother would make this dinner, and all of her family members were invited to come. Visiting guests of theirs would come for lunch and always loved her dinners. They couldn't wait to come back." This makes a lot so you can ask your neighbors, and ask them to bring their friends to dinner with you.

1 small picnic ham or equivalent ham meat
1 head cabbage
6 medium potatoes, chopped into bite-sized pieces

cornmeal dumplings, optional (see Barbara Roberson's collards recipe in the vegetables chapter to find out how to make cornmeal dumplings.)

BOIL THE HAM in water until tender on top of the stove in a stockpot or Dutch oven. Cut the cabbage into eight pieces. Cut up the potatoes, and add both to the pot with the cooked ham. Maintain a low boil until cabbage and potatoes are done. Turn up heat until boiling briskly. Add dumplings. Boil until dumplings are cooked all the way through.

Serves 6 to 8

~ Seafood ~

Easy Crab Cakes

NETTIE KING, **Onslow County**

Eating seafood is a North Carolina passion, and you can get fresh seafood from the coast to the mountains. Seafood is not only delectable, but as a rule it's easy to prepare. Smelling these cakes cook puts (some people would say "sends") me right back to the 1950s and 1960s when my grandparents had a small cottage near Sportsman's Pier in Atlantic Beach. My parents would take my two brothers and me to a short pier on the sound and give us pieces of twine long enough to reach the water. We would tie a little raw bacon to the end and lower the bacon into the brackish water. When we felt a tug, we'd draw out the string and usually find a blue crab attached to the bacon. My father would drop the crabs into a covered bucket until we had enough for dinner. Then my brothers and I would roam barefoot over the dunes trying to avoid the prickly cactus on our way to the beach to collect shells while my mother prepared crab cakes for lunch.

1 pound crabmeat
2 slices bread
2 eggs, beaten
2 tablespoons mayonnaise

2 tablespoons prepared mustard
salt and pepper, to taste
butter, margarine, or oil for frying

CLEAN THE CRABMEAT by removing any cartilage. Crumble the bread into crumbs. Mix crumbs with eggs, mayonnaise, mustard, and seasonings. Gently fold in the crabmeat. Shape into cakes, about 2 tablespoons each. Heat just enough butter, margarine, or oil to cover the bottom of a skillet or griddle. Brown cakes on each side for about 5 minutes. Keep the pan lubricated as you add the remaining cakes.

Serves 4

Fancy Deviled Crab with Sauce

SALLY CREECH, Johnston County

Be sure to remove any cartilage from the crabmeat before mixing it into this tasty dish. "This freezes well," Sally told me. "If you've previously frozen it, bake a little longer."

1½ sticks butter, divided
2 eggs, well-beaten
1 tablespoon Worcestershire sauce
1 tablespoon vinegar
juice of 1 lemon

½ small onion, grated or chopped
    fine
1 pound crabmeat with juice
    reserved
8 saltine crackers, crumbled

PREHEAT OVEN to 425°. Melt 1 stick of the butter in a 1-quart baking dish. Combine the eggs, Worcestershire sauce, vinegar, and lemon juice. Add onion and crabmeat; blend until evenly distributed. Pour into baking dish. Sprinkle all with cracker crumbs and remaining butter. Bake for 20 to 30 minutes.

8 ounces mushrooms	_reserved crabmeat juice_
1 stick (½ cup) butter, divided	_enough milk added to make a_
½ cup all-purpose flour	_quart_
¼ teaspoon salt	_¾ cup mild, white cheese like_
4 shakes pepper	_Swiss or Muenster, grated_

Sauté mushrooms in 2 tablespoons butter. Remove the mushrooms and set aside. Pour the remaining liquid into a bowl. Melt remaining butter over low heat until soft. Add flour, salt, and pepper, stirring until smooth. Gradually add the reserved mushrooms and butter, crabmeat juice, and milk. Blend until smooth. Add cheese as sauce begins to thicken. Pour over the crab cakes when ready to serve.

Serves 4

Crabmeat Quiche

···

FOY ALLEN EDELMAN, Lenoir County

You can make this ahead of time and freeze it. It's great for any meal.

1 unbaked pie shell	*1 tablespoon all-purpose flour*
1 cup Swiss cheese, but cut into	*2 tablespoons butter, melted*
½-inch cubes	*½ teaspoon salt*
½ cup small shrimp, cooked	*dash of pepper*
1 cup crabmeat	*dash of cayenne*
1½ cups light cream	*¼ teaspoon nutmeg*
4 eggs, beaten	*2 tablespoons dry sherry*

PREHEAT OVEN to 375°. Sprinkle the cheese, shrimp, and crabmeat evenly into the pie shell. Combine cream, eggs, flour, butter, salt, pepper, cayenne, and nutmeg. Blend until smooth, then stir in the sherry. When smooth, pour into pie shell. Bake for 40 minutes or until browned and knife inserted in the center of custard comes out clean. Let stand 20 minutes before serving.

Serves 8

Easy Clams on the Half Shell

BROOK DOROSKO, New Hanover County

"When you select your clams," Brook told me, "remember that the smaller they are, the sweeter and tenderer they'll be. To open fresh clams, put them in the freezer, then thaw them for an hour to an hour and a half. They'll open by themselves."

a dozen fresh clams
4 Roma tomatoes, diced
½ cup onion, chopped

3 strips bacon, cut into 1-inch strips

SET OVEN on to broil. Steam your clams for less than five minutes, then they'll open slightly and you can use an oyster or clam knife and lift the top off and loosen each clam. Combine the tomatoes and onions; then spoon them over the clams. Top each one with a couple of strips of the bacon. Broil until the bacon begins to brown. Put it on a nice plate and serve.

Makes 12 clams

Fried Fish

BARBARA HOGGARD, Washington County

Barbara cooks for a crowd at the Senior Center in Washington County. A good way to begin to prepare this dish is to have a friend over to share this fresh delicacy. The skillet, hot oil, and fish will produce a pleasant gurgling sound and a crisp, salty aroma as they cook.

small, fresh fish such as croakers,　*¼ cup all-purpose*
mullets, spots, or other bottom　*salt*
fish, about 2 or 3 per person　*vegetable oil for frying*

Scale, remove heads, and clean fish. Pour about ¾ of an inch of oil into frying pan and heat to medium high. A black iron skillet is the best of all frying pans, particularly for fish or chicken. The most important part of successfully frying fish is getting and keeping the oil at the correct temperature. While the oil is heating, combine the flour and salt in a plastic bag. When the oil just reaches the point of smoking, shake the fish one at time in the flour mixture and place each one in the frying pan. The first fish will tell you if the oil is the right temperature. If it makes a crackling sound as it sinks into the hot oil, the temperature is perfect. If it makes an explosion, the oil it too hot; reduce the heat. If it doesn't make any noise, the oil is too cool; increase the heat. Once the oil's temperature is adjusted, place the rest of the fish in the pan. Brown fish on both sides, then turn heat down to medium to let them cook all the way through; this usually takes about 15 minutes. When they're done, remove the fish and drain on paper until they cool. Serve immediately. You may want to add a little salt, vinegar, lemon juice, or your favorite seafood sauce. This dish is extra good when enjoyed with fresh cole slaw and hot corn bread.

Servings vary according to the size of the fish. You can ask the manager of the seafood market how many you'll need when you purchase them.

Easy Fried Herring

GLADYS UMPHLETT JENNINGS, Pasquotank County

"Daddy [Freeman Umphlett] used to go and drag the seine in the Perquimmans River for the herrings. He would come and clean 'em, and then they'd salt 'em down for the winter. Then they'd always put them in the smoke house. And when mama decided that she wanted herrings – most of the time it was for breakfast because my daddy liked them for breakfast – the night before she'd go out to the smokehouse and she would get the herrings, and she'd wash them and get the bones out of them. And then she would soak them and she might change the water twice before we went to bed. She would soak them overnight. The next morning she patted them dry and mealed them and fried them. And she made a pan of biscuits. That was Daddy's breakfast because he was a farmer and he had to have something to stick to his bones all day, and we got so we enjoyed them too. She always fried them in an iron frying pan.

"The herrings don't run too large. When they get salted, they draw up. And you eat the whole thing. You cook them real crisp. They have the fresh ones at Cannon's Ferry in Chowan County."

Easy Baked Flounder

SUSAN CARSON, Brunswick County

Susan Carson of Southport, known as "Miss Susie" to her neighbors, remembers the town's diet changing during the 1930s from one that frequently included red meat and pork to one that focused on fish, chicken, and starches. "Young boys met the shrimp boats each day and were given the fish that were caught in the nets," she told me. "The boys walked through town in the afternoons selling fish for 25 cents a string. Their catch would find its way onto many tables at suppertime. At that time my mother often fixed deviled eggs, buttermilk biscuits, candied sweet potatoes, cornbread dressing, cornmeal dumplings, cornbread, stewed potatoes (sometimes served with bacon), and bread pudding. These typical dishes were hard-fought sustenance in those days, but they're still tasty favorites that grace our [Brunswick County] tables even now."

small, fresh fish such as croakers, *¼ cup all-purpose*
mullets, spots, or other bottom *salt*
fish, about 2 or 3 per person *vegetable oil for frying*

PREHEAT OVEN to 350°. Grease a 2-quart baking dish. Slash the fish across back. Fill the slices with bacon, then coat it with flour and salt and lay it in the prepared dish. Pour 2 inches of water over the fish. Cover with slices of onion and pour in the tomato puree. Bake 40 or 50 minutes.

Serves 6

Grilled Catfish

REYNOLD ALLEN, Lenoir County

My brother, Reynold Allen, is a gifted sportsman and wonderful cook. He killed a deer with a bow and arrow on his 16th birthday. He told me once that when he goes goose hunting and fires his shotgun, he actually imagines seeing the goose roasted and served on a platter before him!

Any fish is better when you've just pulled it out of the water, but if you can't get to a pond or river, many stores carry farm-raised fish. Here are some ways Reynold prepares catfish. I remember when Reynold served this with fresh, baked pumpkin in the fall. You can find his pumpkin recipe in the vegetable chapter.

"People used to go out and catch catfish, but now they buy them farm raised at the grocery store. Most of what is available around here for consumption are channel catfish. Catfish is an excellent fish to cook, because it has a mild flavor, it takes seasoning very well, and stays firm when cooked unlike a lot of fish species that will fall apart, become flaky and weak as they're cooked, and have to be watched after very carefully lest they fall into the grill or come apart in a pan. Not tough, but (it's) strong enough in its fiber to hold together nicely to cook, and still tender to eat. It is a juicy and easily cooked fish in a variety of ways.

"One way that I cook it is to grill it. I always start with fillets. For a grill, it can be seasoned any way that the cook desires. It can be seasoned with a barbecue sauce. It takes that flavoring well, or it can just be seasoned with a little salt and pepper and lemon juice. One of my favorite ways is to marinate it for some period of time. It doesn't have to be a long time. You can just put it in the marinade for maybe an hour or two before cooking. It soaks up a lot of the flavor, and often you can just use a very simple marinade, something like a zesty Italian salad dressing, and then use it to baste it as it cooks.

"I don't get the grill very hot for fish, of course, but get it warm enough to sizzle it a little bit when it's put on there after marinating it and cook it fairly slowly. Baste it, and turn it every few minutes. Like all fish it doesn't take long to cook it, but you want to cook it long enough to let the flavor into it with the basting. It can tolerate more cook time than other fish without getting too dried out. Experiment with your grill to determine the best temperature and whether to do it covered or uncovered. It's just that simple.

"Another way to cook catfish that I have found to be simple and very tasty is sort of a poaching process and that is to take the fillets, very fresh and very moist, and place them in a pan that is warming up with a couple of pats of butter melting, just enough to coat the pan and give it flavor, or use your favorite oil. You can use olive oil. Put it on low to medium heat, not more than medium. Put the fish in there and season it as desired with salt and pepper or some lemon pepper seasoning or lemon juice, or use Italian dressing for flavoring. Let it cook in its own juices covered slowly for about 35 to 40 minutes. It doesn't take long and the fish is so moist that it will actually poach in its own juices, and still be very moist and have the buttery, oily flavor cooked into it. It has to be checked to make sure that it doesn't overcook. You don't want to boil off the moisture, the water. If you hear it sizzling, it's gone too far. That's a really simple recipe and someone can play with that a little bit, add a little extra to the pan and even make a sauce that can be put over some boiled new potatoes. It's really good!"

Mullet Roast

SAM STAPLES, Camden County

Though my grandfather, Charles Judson Sawyer, was born in Camden County in 1868, I know of no current relations there. Finding cooks in sparsely populated counties proved a challenge; so I searched the history faculty at Elizabeth City State University in adjacent Pasquotank County via the internet until I saw the name of Dr. G. C. Bowman. Dr. Glen Bowman arranged for me to visit the Camden County Senior Center in March of 2004. There I met several local cooks including Sam Staples.

Sam worked for Texaco as a merchant seaman along the east coast for many years until he retired to Camden County, where his family has lived for generations. Several times a year he and friends gather to pull homemade nets in the nearby brackish waterways hoping that the wind will be from the north and bring them some mullets. When the time is right, the fish are cleaned and a hardwood fire made. In days gone by, bay branches were cut from the local trees, soaked in water, and used to spear fish before placing them over the fire, but cutting them quickly denuded the trees of their branches which then quickly disintegrated with use. Now Sam and his friends have developed a special tool, an aluminum shaft approximately 48 inches long with a pointed end that cooks each fish individually as opposed to placing all the fish on a grill. The resulting tasty mullets are accompanied by bowls of sautéed potatoes and onions, baked beans, corn bread, and cucumbers marinated in vinegar. Corn on the cob can also be roasted in the husks while the savory fish cook. Other Camden County favorites are boiled blue crabs, celebrated in the fall with a festival held by the local Shriner's Club, and boiled dinners of vegetables, usually cabbage and potatoes, flavored with meat; streak of fat, streak of lean is preferred.

"(I'm) Sam Phillip Staples, (from) Camden, North Carolina, in the country. Well my father, basically, they used to cook mullets, and no one else around here does it; so what I do is three or four times a summer, we go fishing for mullets in the Pasquotank River or Albemarle Sound. We have a small boat and then sometimes six or eight good friends get together, we pull a net. You always start this the day before. Most of the time you need about thirty mullets. Most of the time we cook fish on a Sunday.

"Okay, now with mullets, what you do with those, you don't cut the heads or anything off. You need about a pound to a pound and a half is a nice mullet to cook. You clean your mullets like your regular fish, but you keep the head on and you pull the gills out, and you have a load of sticks, and the ends of them is like a flat bladed, stainless steel. You slice the fish, then you take the end of the stick, end of the stainless rod and you take the very bottom most slit, that's what you slide up all the way through fish up to his head, let it come out his mouth a little bit. It makes the fish firm and when you're doing this you have a slim side and a fat side on the fish, naturally, when you run it up on him. And then we have a bay leaf bush, and we stuff him with bay leaves, three or four bay leaves. You put pepper and salt on him and make sure your pepper and salt is down in between the slices, and you put right much, not overpowering, but quite a bit because when you're cooking a fish on a fire, naturally, they're fat and a lot of grease drips out. That eliminates a lot of your salt and pepper. But after you do it a certain amount of times you get used to how much to put on there.

"As far as the fire goes, you always start about three hours ahead of time. I use hardwood, like oak or pecan or whichever tree happens to fall in someone's yard. We'll go cut it up; it needs to be seasoned for at least a year, and I keep it under in an old shed like thing. And I let the fire burn down for about three hours. Put right much wood on it; it burns down, because when you get ready to put the fish on it, you don't want any flame, just hot coals. And it's an all-day affair of doing this. I have enough sticks for like fifteen mullets, and you take the sticks and lay them up against the tractor rim. It balances it. You put the end of the sticks in the ground.

Always start cooking with the fat side. If you cook the thin side first and then you turn him over, the meat's done, most of the time, they'll fall off in the fire. Some people take them and put them on a big grid. I don't like to do it that a way because they cook uneven. With an individual stick, you can turn it. Some people like them well done. Some people don't like them. And even though all this stuff is free that we give out, people are particular and that's okay.

"Around this area, Old Trap is basically where they started cooking fish like this, and very few people do it, and most of the time, when we have a cookout, I say I like to get at least 30 fish up to 60, and I call people. A lot of the older people in the county love it, because they don't get them anymore. And they come. Sometimes we have from 30 to 60 people. One particular time we had a rainout. I was going to cook them on a Sunday, and I re-iced everything, waited until the following Wednesday, called everybody, had sixty-some people to show up. I think everybody I called that particular time, everybody came. Most of the time we have 25, maybe 30 people, or whatever. I always have more fish than I call people for, always I don't like to run out.

"The people that come there, the older women, they like to bring something. They don't feel like that they're welcome unless they bring something to eat. So some of them will bring something like potato salad or cornbread. They like to bring cornbread; it's good with mullets. We have like a good layout.

"The only thing I'm responsible for is cooking the fish. And I have a cousin and some friends who give me a hand sometimes with it, because it's a lot of work. I start at probably eight o'clock in the morning, and we finish about five or six in the afternoon, and I have one friend, Jack Berry, he'll bring a fiddle, guitar, two or three sometimes, and they'll play, just sometimes, not all the time.

"You can catch mullets anytime of the year, but I always mess with them, basically, when it's nicer weather. When I was probably six, eight, ten years old, they used to cook mullets at the end of Texas Road. They would set nets then, and when they'd catch enough mullets, they'd come up and cook everything on the shore, wash them in the river shore, and scale them, and all of this. At the time, they would cut sticks out of the woods. It was a night of it. Actually in Old Trap, North Carolina, there was not a whole lot of entertainment. It wouldn't be just a family doing this; it'd be three or four families. It was a good deal. I liked it growing up like that. And then just after everybody got of age, people just didn't have time. It was getting lost. Several people around will cook fish, but I'm set up, I think, fairly well at home, because I have the pit for cooking the mullets. I've got a nice little place out in back, you know, for cleaning fish.

"It was a friend of mine's mother that likes mullets and, well, she didn't have much time to live. She had a cancer, and Dan had told me to make him a mullet. She didn't live only a couple of blocks from me if you consider in the country a couple of blocks. She was down and out; she was still, you know, moving around and all good. I gave him two I cooked, and he took them over there, and she ate them. And she enjoyed it. Dan said 'Oh yeah, those mullets, she enjoyed that.'

"Some of the friends my age, their parents are getting elderly. They all like them. About halfway through everything, I'm just cooking up, then I'm cooking more mullets than they can eat the first time. You know, some people eat two. And then we go ahead and wrap them up in aluminum foil right then and take them to them then. The mullets are nice to eat, but they're not very good to me when they get cold.

"There's no charge for anything, just people getting together. Cooking mullets in Old Trap is a tradition. Somebody has to keep on with the tradition. And my father, when he was younger, somebody had made a record that he knew that was like really in the recording business. They taped him; they made the little forty-five record of him talking about cooking mullets on the river shore. He said in the course, you know, that there was a little boot legging on the side and this, and the record got broke. But see, at the time, when the record was out, people didn't think too much about preserving it. That's the way everything is. When you have stuff right now, you never think that it will get older. But it gets older every day. So anyway, we don't have that anymore."

Picked-up Fish

· ·

FAY KEMP, Dare County

BECKY PAUL, Cartaret County

"This was my grandmother's favorite recipe," Fay told me. "It's what she made anytime we had company." Fay's grandmother combined all her fish, potatoes, and onions into one dish that she served. Becky Paul, from Davis in Cartaret County, told me that her mother was also from Dare County, but made a slightly different version of picked-up fish. "The Ocracoke drum, the big red drum," Becky told me, "that is the favorite fish of Ocracoke. My mother would boil the fish, and have it in a plate. Your potatoes were separate, your onions, boiled eggs chopped, and onions chopped. And when you went to the table, you'd put your potatoes, and then you'd put your fish, and if you wanted onion, egg, bacon bits, and the grease, you fixed it on your plate." "Those sea mullets we've got out there in the sink there are just as good," her husband Alton said. "Alton!" Becky continued, "She would put it on that table; that was her table. She'd have her little dishes of the different things. And we fixed it like we wanted it. Well, when I came up here to Davis and my mother-in-law cooked it, my mother-in-law was from Sea Level, and she cooked like the people here in Davis and Sea Level. She stewed it all together; she stewed her potatoes and onions together, and then she added her fish into that. That's the way they cook it up here. That's like a Core Sound style. On Ocracoke they don't."

Author's Note: These small fish are succulent but have a lot of small bones. If you miss a bone, swallow it by accident, and find it stuck in your throat, don't panic. An old remedy to quickly and safely remove the bone is to take a slice of white bread and soften it into a ball with your fingers. Add a little water, if necessary, to get it to a sticky consistency; the bone will dislodge as you slowly swallow the dough-like bread.

4 or 5 small fish such as croakers, mullets, spots, or other bottom fish, fried

2 or 3 white potatoes, chopped
1 medium onion, chopped

SAVE SOME leftover fried fish or use the recipe for frying fish by Washington County native Barbara Hoggard, in this chapter. When the last fish are removed from the pan, pour off all the oil leaving just enough to cover the bottom of the pan. While the fish are cooling, sauté the chopped potatoes and onion. Then pick the fish off the bones, i.e., remove the skin and carefully separate the meat from the bones. Add the fish meat to the chopped potatoes and onion and serve hot with fresh, sliced tomatoes covered with a generous sprinkling of salt and pepper; peeled, sliced, and chilled cucumbers covered with vinegar; some apple sauce; fresh, fried cornbread, right from the oven, and iced tea.

Serves 2 to 4

Salmon Loaf

RANDY HANES, Davie County

This recipe was compiled by the Green family of Davie County in the 1990s. Their book, Heritage Cookin', is dedicated to their grandparents, Fannie Jones Green (December 23, 1879 – September 14, 1972) and John William Green (January 8, 1873 – November 19, 1939).

2 cups salmon, cooked or canned

2 eggs, well beaten

2 tablespoons butter or margarine, melted

½ cup cornmeal

¼ cup bread or cracker crumbs

salt and pepper, to taste

1 cup buttermilk

1 can (15 ounces) your favorite tomato sauce

PREHEAT OVEN to 425°. Grease a loaf dish or pan well. Flake salmon, remove bones. Combine salmon with eggs, butter, cornmeal, and crumbs. Mix lightly with a fork. Add the salt, pepper, and buttermilk. Blend well, then form into a loaf. Bake for 20 minutes. Top with tomato sauce when serving.

Serves 4 to 6

Real Good Oysters

TOM EPPERSON, Durham County

a little olive oil
1 pint oysters, raw and cleaned
1 package (9 or 10 ounces) frozen
  spinach
garlic clove
small package (8 ounces) Pep-
  peridge Farm or other brand
  stuffing

5 to 6 pieces bacon, softly cooked,
  not crisp
salt and pepper, to taste
some Parmesan or other cheese
butter or margarine
red hot pepper sauce, Tom prefers
  Texas Pete brand hot sauce

PREHEAT OVEN to 350°. Grease each individual well of a tin that makes 12 cupcakes with olive oil. Place one large or two small oysters into each cupcake well. Be certain to remove any shell. Prepare spinach according to directions but adding one clove of garlic while cooking. Place 1 tablespoon of the spinach over each oyster in the muffin tin. Cut each bacon slice into 3 pieces using each to top the oyster and spinach mixture. Sprinkle uncooked stuffing over the spinach, oyster, and bacon. Dot each oyster mixture with a little salt, some Parmesan (or other available) cheese, and a pat of butter or margarine. A dash of red hot pepper sauce is optional. You may substitute cooked shrimp for the oysters. Bake for 8 to 10 minutes, just until oysters are done. Do not overcook.

Serves 4

Scalloped Oysters

JACKI EPPERSON, **Durham County**

I use an 8-inch Pyrex pie plate.
1½ sticks (¾ cup) butter or mar-
* garine, melted and divided*
2 cups breadcrumbs, divided

1 cup oysters, shelled
½ cup cream
salt and pepper, to taste
½ cup oyster liquor

PREHEAT OVEN to 400°. Pour just enough butter into a shallow baking dish to cover the bottom, about ¼ cup. Sprinkle ¾ cup of the breadcrumbs over the butter. Combine oysters, cream, salt, and pepper. When blended, pour into baking dish. Sprinkle remaining breadcrumbs over top. Pour oyster liquor and remaining butter over all. Bake 30 to 35 minutes until bubbly and fragrant.

Serves 2 to 4

Marinated Shrimp

FOY ALLEN EDELMAN, **Lenoir County**

1 large onion, sliced very thin and
* separated into rings*
2 pounds cooked shrimp, deveined
* and shelled*
1 cup vegetable or olive oil

1 cup wine vinegar
¼ cup Worcestershire sauce
dash of red hot pepper sauce
¼ teaspoon garlic salt

Use a bowl that can be refrigerated to pack onion rings and shrimp in alternating layers. Combine oil, vinegar, Worcestershire sauce, red hot pepper sauce, and garlic salt. Blend well, then pour over onions and shrimp. Store in refrigerator for twenty-four hours. Serve cold.

Makes 6 servings

Durham Delicacies – Eggplant with Shrimp

LEONE EPPERSON, Durham County

"Polish eggplants for looks," Mrs. W. S. Griswold of 1540 Hermitage Court writes in her note to Leone. You can make this ahead of time.

3 medium sized eggplants, polished

salt and pepper, to taste

4 tablespoons butter or margarine

1 medium onion, sliced

2 cups shrimp, cooked, cleaned, and minced

¾ cup sour cream

PREHEAT OVEN to 350°. Cut eggplants in half lengthwise. Scoop out the pulp. Parboil the shells and pulp in separate pots for 10 minutes. Remove from heat and drain. Mash the pulp and season. In a skillet over medium heat, melt the butter, and sauté the onion until browned. Remove from heat, and mix the onions with the pulp and shrimp. Blend in the sour cream. Divide the shrimp mixture evenly among the 6 eggplant shells. Heat thoroughly before serving, about 30 minutes.

Serves 6

❧ Game ❧

Roast Bear

. . . .

JENNIE AND JIM VANCE, Avery County

I met the Vance family through Dr. Anne Phillips, a North Carolina history professor who taught me the basics of oral history. Jennie was born in Avery County, where she grew up in a family of thirteen. She and her siblings earned extra money by skinning local cherry bark and drying it. The cured bark was sold to a medicine man from Tennessee named Joe McNeil. The children used the money to purchase a Stella guitar. Jennie and three siblings learned to play, and when she and Jim Vance married in 1946, they formed a bluegrass and country band. Jennie played guitar and bass while Jim performed on many instruments including the mandolin and harp. Their band, High Country Grass, toured Washington, Oregon, Montana, and Idaho for several years before they decided to settle down and start a family. At that point, they got

Jennie and Jim Vance

together with a group of friends for a barn raising; the result is the rustic Music Barn where they perform in Crossnore each Saturday night. High Country Grass traveled to Vietnam and performed forty-three shows in combat zones during the late 1960s.

For Jennie, Jim, their children, and grandchildren, bear, deer, wild turkey, and hog hunting means recreation and good eating. It's also tradition as Jim's grandmother was a Native American, and he has recently been recognized as a member of the Cherokee tribe. And what could possibly go better with wild meat than ramps? These pungent onions taste somewhat like garlic; for mountain folks they're a welcome harbinger of spring each year when their green heads pop up. Ramps are best when they're about two inches long and may be eaten raw, fried, or mixed with eggs or potatoes, though you may find yourself in isolation after consuming them; they create an odor through the skin so offensive that many students are not allowed in school after eating them! Each Memorial Day weekend, visitors from every state and many foreign countries come to the Music Barn when they're celebrated at the Ramps Festival. If the piquant vegetable is too strong for your tastes, Jennie offers an alternative Poor Man's Supper, pinto beans with raw onions and corn bread. If you're really lucky, you might get to try a local dessert that Jennie learned from her mother, Nettie Vance Clark: Apple Bread, a mixture of local apples baked in a bread pan with a crust and lattice top.

Jennie: My name's Jennie Vance and I live in Crossnore.

Jim: Well Ma'am, my grandmother, she was born in Cherokee County, Cherokee, in eighteen and forty and she was Cherokee, but my mother and dad was raised here.

Jennie: I'm seventy-four years old and Jim's seventy-nine and we like to go bear hunting up in Avery County.

Jim: We was raised here and that was our thing in the fall of the year, in the winter, was to take our vacation. After we got our work done, we hunted.

Jennie: And we get a whole lot of people together along with our dogs and we head out to the mountains in the hopes of finding a bear track. If we're lucky enough to kill one, we usually do what the old timers say, we field dress it. We take all the entrails out of it and then when we get home, we turn the water hose on it and wash it out real good, skin it. A lot of times, we cut it up and give each hunter a portion of meat. But if we're close enough to somewhere that they'll process it, we take it and have it processed and wrapped and put in the freezer. And oh boy, how good that is when you get home and you get a big old roast out of that bear.

Jim: I like the roast myself. They always fixed it like that. Sure did!

Jennie: We like to take ours and soak it in vinegar water overnight for a roast. Then we'll put it in the oven. And of course, you've got all of the fat trimmed off the bear meat. Bear fat is really not good. You like to trim off all the fat. Then we put the roast, after we've soaked it overnight, in a little soda and vinegar water. You wash that off and then you put it in a roasting pan just like you would any other roast. But bear meat is dry. So we like to put salt and pepper to taste and if you like garlic, a little garlic salt would be fine. Cover it pretty much with bacon strips because that keeps it from drying out. Of course, we're going to have water in the bottom of the roasting pan. Probably a half an hour to each pound of meat would do it but you can always test it and see if it's well done. And if it's getting too dry on the top, always put a piece of aluminum foil over it and just tent it so it does not dry out. You don't want it to be dry.

Then I do not like to make gravy out of the bear drippings. I usually make my own gravy to go on the top of it. When we do bear meat, we like to use butter as much as possible so we would just make a good, butter gravy to go with this. It's really, really good eating.

I've been in on many, many, many bear chases. We always taught our children as they were growing up, we taught them gun safety. We had two boys and a girl. For their vacation, if they made good grades in school, they could always get out one week out of the year to go bear hunting. My son has killed about forty bear and my daughter has killed four. And my granddaughter has killed three and she's only twelve years old. And I'll let Jim tell you how many he's killed. They call him the grandpappy of all the bear hunters.

Jim: OK, I'm the only one. I'm Grandpa. I've killed ninety-seven. I've killed every one of them a'following my dogs with the exception of one. And we turned on it, we run it about an hour and forty-five minutes, and it came out the same place it went in and I killed it but outside of that I killed all of them a'following my dogs from Michigan, Wisconsin, Florida, Virginia, North Carolina.

Jennie: When you're bear hunting, you like to line all the men up on what we call stands. That's the places you would think that the bear would be coming out if the dogs don't tree it. You don't get scared, or you don't get excited until it's all over, and then you look back and say, "Ooh, I did that or how did I do that?"

Jim: I've never been real scared but the closest I ever come was down on the coast. I shot one night about 11:00 and it was coming straight to me. I emptied a .30-30 in it and it didn't even knock it down. So I put another shell in my gun and I stuck it against his neck and shot him. He fell right on my legs and on my feet, sure did.

Jennie: When we go on a bear hunt and take several people with us like we're going to stay a week at a place and hunt; we have a trial when we come in the evening. If anybody has shot at a bear and they missed it, they get their coattail or their shirttail cut off. A lot of times, the old judge of our hunters, he will make up something and try them for it and get to cut their shirttail off. If somebody shoots at a bear and they miss it, whooo, they get their shirttail cut off and a lot of times if they've got on a new shirt or a new coat, they don't pay no attention to that. They just start cutting it. You get your shirttail, your coattail and all cut off if you shoot at a bear and miss it. And one time we had this guy and he was a city slicker and he come to hunt with us and he had on the most beautiful leather jacket that you have ever seen and a beautiful, beautiful shirt that we would never have wore a'hunting but a city slicker didn't know the difference. And when we had the trial that night, he kept a'looking around and a'looking around and he had shot at a bear with a pistol. Of all the crazy things, he was hunting with a pistol! It come time for us to have the trial that night and they got up, and they cut that beautiful jacket, leather jacket. They cut his beautiful shirt, big, red, beautiful shirt, wool shirt just like anybody else's shirt if they got it at Walmart. We thought that he'd be mad about it but that tickled that man to death that he was in on the hunt and got his coattail and shirttail cut off.

You'd turn the dogs loose and then if you didn't kill the bear that day, you would camp out during the night. We didn't have any walkie-talkie radios or anything and we would camp out. And then the next morning, you'd turn the dogs back loose again and you would hunt the bear until you got him. Now they have walkie-talkie radios.

Jim: The walkie-talkie saves your bear though. If people get on a'talking, and the bear, they're sensitive, they can hear, and that will turn them. They'll go the other way.

Jennie: But back when we first started, you had signals. You would blow your hunting horn. One time would mean, hey, the bear's going down the river, or if you blowed the hunting horn two times, it would mean the bear is going up the river. So all the standers would know which way to go in order to line up to try to kill the bear.

When the bear is killed, field dress it (remove the entrails on site). Wash the bear meat out with water, then trim all of the fat from it. Bear fat does not taste good, so cleaning the meat is very important. Soak the resulting bear roast in soda and vinegar water overnight. When you're ready to cook, rinse the meat off and place it in a large roasting pan. Add salt and pepper to taste. Garlic can also be added if you like. Because the fat has been removed, you must take care so the roast will not be too dry. Cover the whole roast with bacon strips, put water in the bottom of the pan, and watch it carefully. If the meat seems to be drying too quickly, cover it in aluminum foil. Cook 30 minutes per pound of meat at 350°, and test to make sure it's done. Because bear fat is not palatable to most, gravy made with bear drippings is not common. Jennie Vance makes her own simple butter gravy to go with it.

Fried Rabbit with Gravy

ROSE SPEECE, Iredell County

"First you catch the rabbit," says Rose. Or you can find one in the frozen foods section of many grocery stores.

RABBIT	GRAVY
1 rabbit, about 3 pounds cleaned	*remaining drippings*
basin of salt water	*½ cup flour*
4 ounces fatback or suet	*a little bit of milk*
1 cup flour	
1 teaspoon salt	
1 teaspoon black pepper	
lard or Crisco for frying	

SKIN IT and cut it up (cleaning is best done outdoors, since it's a gory job). Rabbit meat tends to be gamey, so the meat must be prepared first: Soak the cut pieces in salt water to remove blood, then parboil in a large pot. Boil the rabbit, along with a piece of salt pork or fatback to "take the wildness out," until the meat is white and tender. Now you are ready to fry the rabbit meat. While the hog lard (you can substitute Crisco if you must) is melting in a deep skillet, mix flour, salt, and pepper, and flour the prepared rabbit. Fry each piece until it is golden brown.

Preparing gravy is an invaluable and subtle art. Heat the residue – or cracklings – of the rabbit in the skillet over low heat. Next add flour and mix until brown. This is the touchy part – the amount of flour you add depends on the amount of oil and cracklings. You're looking for a thick sauce, like a soup roux. Then add a little bit of water or milk, stirring constantly to keep your gravy smooth. Serve fried rabbit and gravy together with biscuits or potatoes.

Serves 6

Roast Rabbit

DOT MOTZINGER, Swain County

"When I was growing up," Dot told me, "wild game was hunted for food as well as for sport. We always had our Thanksgiving dinner at noon each year. After dinner my dad and other male relatives went rabbit hunting while Mother and I cleaned the kitchen and took care of the leftover food. This is our recipe for roast rabbit."

a dressed rabbit, about 3 pounds	*1 teaspoon salt*
2 cups breadcrumbs	*1 small onion, chopped*
¼ to ½ cup hot water	*½ teaspoon pepper*
1 tablespoon butter, softened to	*1 tablespoon sage*
room temperature	*6 strips bacon*

SOAK RABBIT in cold water for a few hours. When ready to cook, preheat oven to 350°. Make dressing by combining breadcrumbs, just enough hot water to moisten the breadcrumbs, butter, salt, onion, pepper, and sage. Stuff rabbit with dressing. Cover with bacon and bake, basting often. Bake for about 30 minutes per pound. Meat will be tender when done.

Serves 4 to 6

Duck with Orange

RICK HAMILTON, Wake County

5 to 6 pound duck, cleaned
2 tablespoons butter, divided
4 tablespoons all-purpose flour,
*   divided*

1 cup orange marmalade
salt and pepper, to taste
1 medium onion, peeled
3 oranges

PREHEAT OVEN to 450°. Simmer the neck and giblets of the duck in just enough water to cover it for about 30 minutes. Chop giblets and discard neck. Melt 1 tablespoon butter, and stir in 1 tablespoon of the flour. Add stock from giblets and the marmalade; blend, then set off burner. Season duck inside and out with salt and pepper, and dredge lightly with remaining flour. Put onion in the cavity. Peel one of the oranges, separate the sections, and put in cavity. Secure the opening with skewers. Put onto a rack in a shallow roasting pan and bake for 30 minutes. Reduce heat to 350°, and pour the marmalade gravy over the duck. Cook for another hour, basting occasionally. Remove duck from oven. Take most of the fat from the pan by pouring it off the top. Melt 1 tablespoon of butter and 1 tablespoon flour in a saucepan. When well blended, make gravy by adding the remaining pan drippings. Use the remaining two oranges as decoration when serving.

Serves 8

Doves Deluxe

TOM EPPERSON, Durham County

Tom Epperson is a native of Durham, an enthusiastic cook, an Eagle Scout leader, and an avid outdoorsman. Dove hunting season in North Carolina begins in September and lasts until the middle of January. Tom frequently hunts on a friend's property in Orange County during January after the deer season has ended. He freezes fresh, picked, and cleaned doves in water to preserve the flavor. Tom says that "happy" onions are those that have been sautéed until they're soft. Tom's recipe can also be used for quail and squab, which you can purchase in the frozen foods section of many grocery stores.

12 picked and cleaned doves, *bacon*
    preferably with wings on *1 clove garlic*
1 onion, chopped, divided *3/4 cup flour*
Worcestershire sauce *1 can chicken broth*
dashes of red (cayenne) and black *splash of beer, red or white wine,*
    pepper, salt *optional*
bacon grease from 5 to 6 slices of

You will need two separate saucepans, one to be used for simmering the doves, the other to be used for making a roux, or flour paste, that will eventually make the dove gravy. In the first saucepan, cover the doves with water, adding ½ chopped onion, some Worcestershire sauce, a dash of red pepper, a dash of black pepper, and some salt. Simmer over medium heat for an hour and a half until the meat begins to separate from the bone. Turn heat to low while you make the roux. In a second saucepan, sauté half of the chopped onion in the bacon grease with a clove of garlic, some salt, black and red pepper, and 1 tablespoon of Worcestershire sauce. Sauté over medium to high heat until the onions clarify, usually 5 to 6 minutes. When onions are "happy," reduce heat to medium, and stir some of the flour into the grease. This will make a thick, rich paste. Open and pour some of the chicken broth gradually into the, paste stirring constantly to keep it smooth. Continue cooking over medium heat while you add a splash of beer, red, or white wine. This will create a delicious aroma and flavor. Continue adding flour and chicken broth until a smooth paste is ready. This usually takes 5 to 10 more minutes after all the flour and broth are added. The resulting roux will be slightly brown, thick, and glossy. Remove doves from the first saucepan, leaving the broth. Then add the roux to the dove broth, turning up the heat to medium, and keep stirring until thick gravy develops. Doves may be combined with the gravy or served separately. This savory dish is beautiful when garnished with parsley and a great companion for wild rice, broccoli, hot cornbread, and red wine.

Serves 4

ᏕᎧ Vegetarian ᏕᎧ

Lentil Loaf

KELAINE ZIMMERMAN HAAS, **Rowan County**

"I think this is a good alternative to traditional meatloaves. It's delicious," Kelaine told me. "I tried it for the first time, because I was looking for a vegetarian option for comfort/soul food. Even if someone isn't vegetarian, this is a great dish to have with mashed potatoes and green beans. I also like to use it when I am cooking for a group that includes people who do and don't eat meat. It's basically a crowd pleaser all around. Adding some Italian spices and garlic, and trading the cheddar cheese for mozzarella makes for some really amazing no-meatballs."

1 cup breadcrumbs
1 package (1 to 1.1 ounces) onion
  soup mix
1 egg, beaten
1 cup cheddar cheese, grated
1 onion, chopped
2 tablespoons butter, softened
¾ cup lentils cooked until soft

SAUCE

½ cup catsup
2 tablespoons mustard
2 tablespoons brown sugar

PREHEAT OVEN to 350°. Combine breadcrumbs, soup mix, egg, cheese, onion, and butter. Blend until smooth; then mix in the lentils. Spoon mixture into a loaf dish or pan, approximately 8- x 4- x 2.5-inches. Bake for 35 to 40 minutes. Make the sauce by combining catsup, mustard, and brown sugar together and beating until smooth. Remove lentil loaf; cover the top with sauce, and bake for an additional 10 minutes.

Serves 4 to 6

Bean Bread

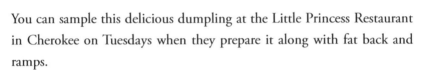

EMILY SMITH, Qualla Boundary
(also known as the Cherokee Reservation)

You can sample this delicious dumpling at the Little Princess Restaurant in Cherokee on Tuesdays when they prepare it along with fat back and ramps.

4 cups cooked pinto beans, unseasoned	*2 cups milk*
1 cup cornmeal	*1 egg, beaten*
½ cup all-purpose flour	*dried corn shucks*
2 teaspoons baking powder	*a pot of boiling water*

BOIL PINTO BEANS as though to eat, but do not season. Combine cornmeal, flour, baking powder, milk, and egg. Add beans to corn meal mixture bit by bit, until you have stiff dough. Wet hands in cold water to form balls about 1½ inches in diameter. Flatten and wrap balls with the dried corn shucks; you may need to tie them with twine. Boil until cooked all the way through, usually about an hour. Remove and drain.

Serves 4 to 6

Easy Plain Omelet

LEONE EPPERSON, Durham County

I lived in Cheltenham, England from 1971 to 1972. A friend and I often drove to Bath (the one in England, not the one in Cartaret County, NC) to buy cloth from the Laura Ashley shop. We always ate lunch at a café called The Mad Hatter. It served only omelets made from this basic recipe, but offered the most delicious variations: sausage, cheese, sautéed vegetables, smoked salmon, crab, or ham; the combinations were endless, and all delicious! Fluffy omelets like this recipe are really easy to make. The method includes pouring the eggs into a skillet on top of the stove first, then placing it in a preheated oven to let it cook all the way through. I find that the fresher the eggs, the fluffier the result.

4 eggs, separated	*1 tablespoon hot water*
salt and pepper, to taste	*2 tablespoons butter or margarine*

fillers for your omelet may include your favorite grated cheese, sautéed vegetables, chopped ham, salmon, or whatever your imagination suggests

PREHEAT OVEN to 350°. Beat egg yolks until thick and lemon colored. Add seasonings and water. Beat egg whites until stiff and dry; gently fold them into the yolk mixture. Butter the sides and bottom of a skillet or omelet pan; then place the pan on burner set over medium heat. When the butter has melted, pour in the eggs. Leave on the burner until the bottom of the omelet has browned. Use a spatula to fold the omelet in half. Remove from burner and place in the oven until it has cooked through, usually 10 to 15 minutes. I usually start checking it at 12 minutes by pressing the top gently. When it springs back, it's done.

Serves 2

Easy Cheese Soufflé

ELIZABETH (LIB) JONES WATKINS, Bertie County

This is really a mock soufflé that never fails, not a real one where you have to separate the eggs, beat the whites, and carefully fold into a roux, or it will surely fall. Instead, you can make this ahead for your cheese lovers. "Add 1 cup of sautéed mushroom for a one-dish supper," Lib says in a note.

8 slices of your favorite bread
1 stick (½ cup) butter or marga-rine, softened to room tempera-ture
3 eggs, beaten

2 cups milk
2 teaspoons dry mustard
salt, pepper, and cayenne to taste
1½ cups of your favorite cheese, grated

PREHEAT OVEN to 350°. Grease a 2-quart baking dish. Cut the edges off the bread. Liberally butter each slice. Blend the eggs, milk, mustard, salt, pepper, and cayenne together until smooth. Lay slices of the bread in bottom of prepared dish. Sprinkle with cheese. Repeat until all the bread and cheese are used. Pour the egg mixture over all. Be sure you refrigerate this if you make it ahead. When ready to serve, bake for 30 minutes. Does it get any easier?

Serves 6 to 8

Easy Baked Potato Main Dish

FOY ALLEN EDELMAN, Lenoir County

I grew up in a frugal household and still enjoy making the most of the foodstuffs available to me. At the end of the week, I often have a few odds and ends left in the fresh vegetable bin. This quick dish is one of my favorite ways to make a tasty and nutritious meal without another trip to the store. You can also use cooked vegetables, but you won't need to steam them, just warm them up. I often use broccoli, onions, cauliflower, carrots, mushrooms, squash, asparagus, tomatoes, green, yellow, red, and orange peppers.

¾ cup of cheese sauce per serving (see recipe in Chapter 7: Gravies, Marinades, Sauces, and Salad Dressings)
1 baking potato for each serving

a variety of your favorite vegetables
pepper and seasoned salt, to taste
paprika, optional
chopped parsley, optional

PREPARE CHEESE SAUCE and keep it warm. Pierce the potatoes, then bake them either in a conventional oven (45 minutes at 400°, 60 minutes at 350°, or 90 minutes at 325°) or in a microwave oven (1 medium to large potato takes from 8 to 12 minutes at full power).

Cut raw vegetables into pieces about 2 inches long. Place them in a steamer over medium-high heat for 5 to 10 minutes, depending on how cooked you like your vegetables. Remove potatoes from oven and put them on individual plates. Drain the vegetables, evenly distribute them over the potatoes, and season. Pour cheese sauce over each potato filled with vegetables. Sprinkle with paprika and garnish with parsley. Bon appétit!

Each potato serves 1

Sandwich Loaf

LEONE EPPERSON, Durham County

Leone credits Ethel Stanard with this recipe. "Cut crust from Pullman loaf of bread," reads the head note. A Pullman loaf refers to a basic loaf of white bread that is rectangular in shape. Perhaps it is named "Pullman" because it was easy to stack and store on the many Pullman cars that traveled North Carolina's railroads during the 1920s. Any unsliced loaf of bread will work for this recipe. "Something to drink and an ice course makes a nice luncheon," suggests Ethel Stanard.

1 loaf of unsliced bread
1 small onion, diced
1 tablespoon green pepper, chopped, divided
1½ cups mayonnaise, divided
3 hard cooked eggs, peeled and sliced

½ cup stuffed olives, chopped or ½ cup tapanade
1 cup English walnuts, chopped
2 packages (8 ounces each) cream cheese, softened
½ cup lemon juice

CUT THE BREAD lengthwise in the middle, then cut each half through the center making 4 long slices. Combine the onion, half of the green pepper, and half of the mayonnaise. Spread evenly on bottom slice;

then arrange the eggs and bacon on top. Add a slice of bread on top. Combine the olives or tapanade with the walnuts, the remaining green pepper, and the remaining mayonnaise. Spread on top of bread. Add another slice of bread. Blend the cream cheese with the lemon juice and spread the entire loaf with the mixture. Top with the remaining bread. Cut the layered loaf into 1½ inch slices to serve.

Serves 8

Potpies &
Skillet Dinners

L ike memories of happy events that replay over and over again in your mind after they happen, memories of favorite foods stick around for generations. Imagine lustrous gravy flowing out of vents in lightly browned pastry, skillets filled with hot combinations of meat and vegetables, dishes that infuse your home with mouth-watering aromas, luring hungry family and friends to your table. This chapter includes satisfying dishes often made from leftovers imaginatively refashioned into wholesome family meals.

That tasty marriage between pastry and meat filling, the potpie, has a long and esteemed history in this state. The oldest published cookbook I know of that is authored by a North Carolinian is Dixie Cookery. It appeared in June of 1867 and sold for 38 cents. The following recipe appears on page 24:

CHICKEN PIE
Maria Massey Barringer, Concord, 1867

Cut up the chickens into joints, and season them with salt, pepper, and parsley. If they are old, parboil them a few minutes, and save the water to put in the pie. Make rather a rich paste [crust], and cover the bottom and sides of a deep dish with it. Then put in alternate layers of chicken, six hard-boiled eggs cut in slices, butter, pepper, celery, and a little flour from your dredging-box. Fill the dish two-thirds full of cold water, and add half a teacup of cream or milk. Put on a top paste, and close the pie around the edge, and make an opening in the middle with a knife. It will require about an hour to bake. A few slices of ham are an addition liked by many persons. If oysters are in season, they are nice, put in alternate layers with the chicken.

An even simpler rendition of chicken potpie appears in a newspaper clipping preserved in Leone Epperson's handmade recipe collection compiled in Durham during the 1920s:

Cook chicken until it falls from bones and mince into fine pieces. Line a pan with a crust not very rich and put in chicken seasoned with salt and pepper and several crackers broken into small pieces. Pour broth over this and dot with bits of butter. Put on top crust and bake until very brown. Also use with rabbits or pigeons.

It doesn't take complicated words to describe a simple dish. Carolyn Goff of Harnett County uses this basic yet irresistibly good recipe. "Boil chicken," she told me. "Take off bone. Mix 2 cans broth and 1 can cream of chicken soup. Bring to a boil. Put chicken in pie dish lined with pastry. Take [and serve up]."

Potpies are just as popular today as in generations past, and there are several variations to try. From Buncombe County we get the recipe for pastry; from Vance County, a traditional chicken with vegetable pie favored by Donna Matthews Saad. Rebecca Neff contributes a family recipe called Florence's Potpie packed with chicken and flavored with vinegar. Alice Sharpe from farther east in Hertford County creates a six-ingredient pan pie that's so large it can serve ten people. I make Thanksgiving and Christmas holiday flavors last by turning turkey scraps into rich potpies.

Skillet dinners have many advantages: They're often simple to make, supply plenty to share, and end with only one pan to clean. These dinners can be as straightforward as spaghetti or as elaborate as shrimp almond. Again, chicken flavored dinners are widely enjoyed. One of the skillet dinners that I remember from childhood is sometimes called a "slowdown." Place a cut-up chicken in a skillet with a little seasoning. Cover it with water, put a lid over it, and set the burner on low. Let it simmer all day until the meat falls off the bone. Remove bones and skin before ladling the tender chicken and savory broth into a low bowl lined with slices of white bread or crushed saltine crackers. Versions of this dish date back for generations, though they were not often recorded on paper, but passed along in the oral tradition. It's probably one of the simplest recipes there ever was and is a way to stretch food during hard times.

Another favorite group of skillet dinner recipes involves mixing ground beef with other ingredients to produce a hearty result, like this one:

ALL-IN-ONE SPECIAL
Bobbie Jackson (Northside neighborhood), Orange County

1 pound ground beef
1 medium green sweet pepper, chopped
½ medium onion, chopped
1 tablespoon shortening
1 (10 ¾ oz.) can tomato soup
1 soup can water
1 can (8 ounces) corn, drained
4 drops Tabasco hot sauce
1 cup noodles
dash of pepper

Brown beef with green pepper and onion in shortening. Stir to separate meat particles. Pour off drippings; add remaining ingredients. Cover; cook over low heat 20 minutes. Stir now and then.

From a coastal plain recipe for easy hash to a sophisticated dish for shrimp Creole bonanza from Halifax County, North Carolina cooks have combined a diversity of charms in their skillets over the years. You'll find two spaghetti sauces, one traditional and a lighter white clam sauce also served over pasta, included in this chapter. From the coastal plain we get smothered chicken; from the Piedmont, a broccoli and chicken skillet; from the tidewater, shrimp and grits. Wherever you find them, they're popular crowd pleasers.

❧ Potpies ❧

Double Piecrust - for use with Potpies

MARGUERITE HUGHEY, Buncombe County

This makes a perfect crust for potpies. Margaret Fort gave this handwritten recipe to Marguerite in October of 1997.

2 cups all-purpose flour
1 teaspoon salt
½ cup vegetable oil

¼ cup milk
additional all-purpose flour for
* rolling out*

MIX THE FLOUR with salt in a small mixing bowl. Combine the oil and milk together. Make a well in the middle of the flour mixture. Pour in the combined oil and milk. Mix with a fork until a ball forms. Sprinkle flour on waxed paper. Divide dough in half. Roll out on waxed paper.

Makes 2 crusts

Chicken Potpie

DONNA MATTHEWS SAAD, Vance County

Donna gives credit to her friend, Andie, for this easy and tasty chicken pie.

1 stick (½ cup) butter
*3 cups chicken, cooked and cut
  into bite-sized pieces*
*2 cans (15 ounces each) Veg-All,
  drained*
1½ cups chicken broth
*1 can (10.75 ounces) cream of
  chicken soup*

*1 can (10.75 ounces) cream of
  celery soup*

TOPPING INGREDIENTS
1 stick (½ cup) butter, melted
1½ cup Bisquick
¾ cup milk

PREHEAT OVEN to 350°. Melt butter in a 9 x 12-inch baking dish. Combine chicken, Veg-All, chicken broth, chicken and celery soups in a saucepan. Heat over medium until completely blended. Pour evenly into prepared baking dish. Make the topping by combining the butter, Bisquick, and milk. Blend well, then sprinkle over chicken mixture. Bake 1 hour.

Serves 6 to 8

Florence's Chicken Pie

REBECCA NEFF, Forsraryth County

PIECRUST

3 cups all-purpose flour
½ teaspoon baking powder
1 teaspoon salt
1 cup Crisco

1 egg
1 tablespoon fresh lemon juice
5 tablespoons cold water

PREPARE DOUGH for two crusts. Combine 3 cups flour, ½ teaspoon baking powder, and 1 teaspoon salt. Add 1 cup Crisco and blend. Mix together egg, lemon juice, and water. Add the egg mixture to the dry ingredients and mix lightly to form a soft dough. Wrap in waxed paper or plastic wrap and chill for at least an hour.

FILLING

3 to 5 pounds chicken
salt and pepper

1 tablespoon vinegar
2 to 3 tablespoons butter

REMOVE GIBLETS from chicken before cutting it into pieces; season pieces with salt and pepper. Place chicken pieces in a skillet, cover with water, and stew gently over low to medium heat until tender. Add vinegar; this will act as a tenderizer. Cool chicken. Reserve the broth. Remove skin and bones from meat and set aside.

PREHEAT OVEN to 400°. Divide dough in half. Roll out bottom crust and place in 10-inch pie plate. Put chicken in crust and dot it with butter. Warm half of the broth over low to medium heat, then gradually stir in just enough flour to thicken it. Continue stirring until smooth. Pour the thickened broth over the chicken and cover with top crust. Bake at 400º for 15 minutes. Reduce heat to 350º, and continue baking for another 45 minutes.

Serves 6

Sharpe's Chicken Pan Pie

ALICE POWELL SHARPE, Hertford County

Chicken pan pies are potpies with almost no vegetables.

young roaster or fryer, 2 to 2½
  pounds
1 medium onion, chopped
1 teaspoon of garlic
2 tablespoons of poultry seasoning

1 package of thin rolled piecrust
1 can (10.75 ounces) cream of
  chicken soup or cream of mush-
  room soup

PREHEAT OVEN to 350°. Wash, clean, and cut up the chicken, then steam it in a pot on top of the stove for 20 to 30 minutes. Take the pot off the stove. Remove the chicken, reserving the broth, and place in a baking pan approximately 14 x 10 x 2-inches. Add the onion, garlic, and poultry seasoning. Cover with strips of pastry. Pour the soup over the pastry. Bake for about 30 minutes, basting pastry with reserved chicken broth after 15 minutes. Pie is done when the pastry is crispy and brown.

Serves 10

Turkey or Chicken Potpie

FOY ALLEN EDELMAN, Lenoir County

Long ago in Lenoir County where I was raised, local people used homemade lard for cooking. We used it for frying chicken, making biscuits and piecrusts, flavoring vegetables, and in many other ways. Lard gave foods a deliciously sweet, smoky flavor but contained unhealthy fats. Gradually over the years, cooks replaced lard with healthier vegetable shortenings and oils. I miss the flavor of lard and substitute a few ounces of chopped ham to add savor to an otherwise mild combination of ingredients. These potpies freeze well, but need to be completely thawed before baking.

pastry to line a pie shell and for a top crust

½ cup ham, cooked and chopped, optional

1½ cups turkey or chicken, cooked, skinned, deboned, and chopped into bite-sized pieces

1½ cups of your favorite mixed vegetables, cooked

1½ cups gravy, see recipe in the Gravies chapter

½ cup cheddar cheese, grated

¼ cup butter or margarine, cut into pats, optional

PREHEAT OVEN to 350°. Line a deep-dish pie plate with one of the crusts. Spread the ham evenly in the bottom of the pastry, then spread the chicken and vegetables. Pour the gravy over all. Sprinkle the cheese on top, then dot with butter or margarine. Fit the top crust over the pie; trim the edges; make slits in the crust. Place pie dish on a cookie sheet. Bake until crust is golden brown and gravy is bubbly, 30 to 40 minutes.

Serves 6

Easy Squirrel or Quail Pie

RETHA SUMMERS DURHAM, **Wilkes County**

"This was so delicious." Retha said. "[When I was a little girl] we would kill our own squirrels. You could make this with squirrels, quails, or rabbits. Lunch was dinner then, at 12 noon. We would sit around the table at home and talk. Daddy would talk about the experiences he had had going out to hunt. I had two sisters and two brothers. We had a long bench we sat on at the table. Mama and Daddy had chairs. My place was always beside Daddy. He sat at the end, and I sat right beside him. I liked that, because he spoiled me. Mama did most of the cooking, but Daddy helped her. After we ate, Mama and Daddy would go out to sit on the front porch. My sisters and I would have to wash the dishes and clean up. We would get in the kitchen and sing. All we knew at the time was religious songs, because that's what we learned at church. We cooked in a wood stove, and Mama had a warming closet on the stove. What was leftover was put up there in the warming closet and saved for supper. We had a garden, and nobody in the world could cook pinto beans like Mama could. She put those things on and parboiled them and then she washed them and put them in a pot with fatback. And you had to have cornbread. Daddy always used the white corn meal, coarse ground at Union Grove Mill. Daddy's favorite thing to have when we had company to drop in and Mama didn't have anything cooked was ham, gravy, fried eggs, and biscuits, that good old gravy. She made that red eye gravy. She put a little bit of coffee in it to give it color and that was delicious. Mama and Daddy were the type of people, when you came in their house, they treated you like one of the family. They wanted you to eat something. They weren't satisfied if you didn't eat something!"

*4 squirrels or quail, cleaned, or 1
    rabbit cut into pieces
boiling water
4 ounces of fatback, butter, or
    margarine*

*2 unbaked piecrusts
salt and pepper, to taste
¼ cup all-purpose flour*

CLEAN THE SQUIRRELS, removing the head, hide, and entrails. Cut off the legs and soak them with the body in cold salt water for about an hour. Then, put them in a covered saucepan on top of the stove with the fatback; simmer until the meat is tender. Preheat oven to 350°. Remove the meat, reserving the cooking broth. Line a pie plate with one of the crusts. Separate the meat from the bones; place the meat in the pie pan. Salt and pepper it. Heat the reserved broth over low to medium heat. Gradually stir the flour into the reserved broth. Continue stirring until broth thickens. Pour over the meat. Cover the meat and gravy with the other piecrust. Bake until the crust is brown. Serve immediately.

Serves 6

❧ Skillet Dinners ❧

Smothered Chicken

· ·

ELLA BRADSHAW, Lenoir County

This is an old stand-by that's so easy it can be passed along without ever writing it down.

"We serve this for breakfast with rice and biscuits," says Ella.

> *1 whole chicken, cut into pieces*   *½ to ¾ cup flour*
> *½ to 1 cup lard or shortening*   *salt and pepper, to taste*

CLEAN AND WASH chicken pieces. Put a full-sized iron frying pan over medium heat with just enough lard or shortening to cover the bottom. As soon as lard is melted and begins to crackle, lay in the chicken pieces. Let them brown on each side until they're about half done. Add a little water, place the lid on the pan, turn the heat down to low, and let it simmer for 20 to 30 minutes. Continue cooking until the pieces are done all the way through. When the chicken is tender and a fork goes all the way through a piece, it's done. Remove the chicken from the pan to make the gravy. Mix ½ to ¾ cup flour in a little water. Stir until the mixture is smooth. Pour the flour and water into the pan, heated over low to medium heat, to make gravy. Continue cooking until gravy thickens, usually in 5 to 10 minutes. Replace the chicken, season to taste with salt and pepper, and set the table.

Serves 8

Chicken and Broccoli Skillet Dinner

JACOB KARRIKER, **Stanly County**

1 tablespoon vegetable oil	*¼ teaspoon paprika*
4 boneless chicken breast halves	*¼ teaspoon black pepper*
1 can (10.75 ounces) cream of chicken soup	*2 cups instant white rice*
1½ cups water	*2 cups fresh or frozen broccoli flowerets*

HEAT THE OIL in a skillet over medium to high heat. When hot, add
the chicken breast, brown on both sides, then remove and drain. Turn
the heat down to between low and medium. Add the soup, water,
and seasonings. Stir and gradually heat to boiling. Pour in the rice
and broccoli. Top with chicken. Season with additional paprika and
pepper to taste. Cover. Cook on low heat for 5 minutes, or until cooked
through. Serve immediately.

Serves 4

Skillet Meal

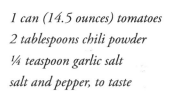

JANET MANUEL, **Martin County**

½ cup shortening	*1 can (14.5 ounces) tomatoes*
1 large onion, diced	*2 tablespoons chili powder*
1 pound ground beef	*¼ teaspoon garlic salt*
1 cup white rice	*salt and pepper, to taste*
1 can (15 ounces) red kidney beans	

MELT SHORTENING in large frying pan. Sauté onion and beef until browned. Add rice, beans, tomatoes, and seasonings. Blend well. Cover and cook over low to medium heat for 30 to 45 minutes or until rice is done.

Serves 4 to 6

Beef Stroganoff
• •

ARAMINTA PIERCE BLOWE, Halifax County

All you need for a meal is this tasty stroganoff, some toasted bread, and a simple green salad. It is a hearty meal with only one pot to clean up. If you prefer vegetarian, leave out the meat, and add another 2 cups of mushrooms.

1 stick (½ cup) butter or
   margarine
1 pound ground sirloin or
   hamburger
1 onion, chopped
3 cups uncooked narrow noodles
3 cups tomato juice
¼ cup Worcestershire sauce

dashes of salt and pepper
2 teaspoons celery salt
1 cup sour cream
1 cup mushrooms, cleaned and
   sliced, optional
2 tablespoons parsley, chopped
2 teaspoons thyme

IN A LARGE skillet, melt the butter over medium heat. Add the beef and onion. Stir until browned; pour off the excess grease into a container. Return skillet to burner and lay the uncooked noodles on top of the beef and onion mixture. Pour in the tomato juice, Worcestershire sauce, salt, pepper, and celery salt. Cover the skillet and simmer. Stir occasionally until noodles are tender, about 20 minutes. Turn down the heat to low and add sour cream, mushrooms, parsley, and thyme.

Serves 6

Ed's Hash

···

CAROLYN GOFF, Harnett County

2 pounds lean, bottom butt pork roast	*salt and pepper, to taste*
	2 sticks (1 cup) butter
2 pounds bone-in chuck roast	*2 cubes beef bouillon*
2 medium onions, chopped	*¼ cup prepared mustard*

PLACE BOTH roasts in a stockpot with an onion. Salt and pepper and cover with 2 inches of water. Simmer on top of stove until tender. This usually takes 3 to 4 hours. Remove from heat; take out the meat, reserving the broth. When the meat cools, remove any fat and bones, then pull it apart into strips. When the broth is cool, remove any fat from the top. Add the butter, onions, bouillon, and mustard. Simmer, stirring often, until well blended. Put the strips of meat back into the broth, heat well, and serve.

Makes 2 quarts

Easy Sloppy Joes

MARGUERITE HUGHEY, Buncombe County

1 pound ground beef
1 teaspoon celery seed
1 onion, chopped
salt and pepper, to taste

1 teaspoon chili powder
½ cup catsup
3 teaspoons vinegar

COMBINE all ingredients in a skillet on top of the stove. Let simmer for about 30 minutes. Pour over split hamburger buns to serve.

Serves 4

Sweet and Savory Beans with Wieners

MARGUERITE HUGHEY, Buncombe County

A note on this recipe says "Ruth 1983."

½ cup celery, chopped
½ cup green pepper, chopped
¼ cup butter
½ pound wieners, sliced into
* rounds*
¼ cup brown sugar

¼ cup soy sauce
¼ cup catsup
1 tablespoon vinegar
1 tablespoon molasses, optional
1 teaspoon cornstarch
2 cups canned pork and beans

SAUTÉ celery and green pepper until soft in buttered skillet over medium heat. Add wieners, brown sugar, soy sauce, catsup, vinegar, and molasses.

When hot, sprinkle the mixture with cornstarch and stir until it thickens slightly. Add pork and beans. Continue cooking until all is hot throughout.

Serves 4

Liver Nips
....

CAROLYN GOFF, Harnett County

"You can use chicken livers but calf's liver is the best," Carolyn told me.

½ cup liver, chopped
1/8 cup suet, chopped
1 medium onion, chopped
2 eggs, beaten
2 cups all-purpose flour

1 teaspoon salt
½ teaspoon baking powder
8¾ cups beef broth or consommé, divided

COMBINE liver, suet, and onion in a mixing bowl. Add eggs. Combine flour, salt, and baking powder. Little by little add the flour mix to the liver mixture; then slowly blend in ¾ cup beef broth until you have medium stiff dough. Heat the remaining beef broth until almost boiling. Spoon in the liver mixture by tablespoons. Cook until dumplings are cooked all the way through, 20 to 30 minutes, and a nice thick gravy is formed by the beef broth.

Serves 4

Spaghetti Sauce

LEONE EPPERSON, Durham County

Leone attributes this recipe to Lois L. Fowler.

1½ large onions, chopped
½ cup vegetable oil
1 pound ground beef
1 green pepper, chopped, optional
2 cloves garlic, minced, optional
3 tablespoons Worcestershire sauce
2 teaspoons red hot pepper sauce

dash of cinnamon
1 can tomato puree or tomato sauce
¾ can tomato paste
1 cup water
salt and pepper
1 cup mushrooms, chopped

IN A LARGE skillet, sauté onions in oil until soft; pour out excess oil, then add meat and brown while you stir the meat with the onions. Add remaining ingredients, blend well, and then simmer until thick, about 2 hours.

Serves 6

Alice's Easy Clam Sauce

KAREN GOINS, Scotland County

"I learned this from my mother, Alice Raymous," Karen told me. "You can add as much as a can of clams per person if you like."

vegetable or olive oil
2 stalks celery, washed and
   chopped
1 clove fresh garlic, minced
bunch of fresh parsley, rinsed and
   chopped

1 or 2 cans (6.5 ounces each)
   clams, minced
your favorite spaghetti noodles

"I put some oil in the frying pan," Karen explained. "I chop up celery real fine and a bud of fresh garlic, very fine. It's time consuming. Fry celery and garlic in vegetable oil. Garlic always smells good frying. After it starts to brown a little bit, put some fresh parsley in it. I use (6.5 ounces) canned clams, minced. Dump them with the juice into your garlic, celery, and parsley. You can see the little brown bits of garlic and celery. Boil your spaghetti. Pour the clam sauce over it, and it is divine."

Serves 4 to 6

Shrimp and Grits

NETTIE KING, Onslow County

3 tablespoons butter
3 tablespoons all-purpose flour
3 strips bacon
3 tablespoons virgin olive oil
2 large sweet onions
6 to 8 cloves garlic, crushed
1 cup mushrooms, cleaned and
   sliced

1 red pepper, seeds removed and
   minced
2 pounds fresh shrimp, peeled and
   uncooked
6 cups cooked grits, hot
2 cups sharp cheddar cheese
1 cup cream

MELT BUTTER in a saucepan. Add flour and cook over low heat until mixture is smooth, usually about 5 minutes; then remove from burner and set aside. Fry the bacon. When crisp and brown, remove from burner, drain, and chop into small pieces. Pour bacon grease out and discard. Rinse skillet and dry, then heat the olive oil in it hot enough to sauté the onions and garlic. When the onions are tender, add mushrooms and red pepper. Stir until mushrooms are tender. Add bacon, flour mixture, and shrimp. Sauté all until shrimp are pink and just cooked through. Add cheese to hot grits. Stir until melted, then blend in cream. Serve shrimp over grits to an audience that will sigh when they eat it, and then faint with satisfaction.

Serves 4 to 6

Easy Shrimp Creole

SALLY CREECH, Johnston County

"Do not substitute corn or canola oil," Sally said. "The flavor is not the same. You can also make this dish with chicken by cutting up 4 boneless skinless breasts into bite sized pieces, but it takes a little longer to cook."

3 to 4 tablespoons safflower or peanut oil
1 teaspoon salt
1 bay leaf
1 clove garlic, minced
dash of red hot pepper sauce
1 tablespoon Chef Paul Magic (or your favorite) seafood seasoning

1 pound steamed shrimp, deveined and cut into bite-sized pieces
3 to 4 ounces mushrooms, cleaned and sliced into bite-sized pieces
1 can (28 ounces) stewed tomatoes
1 can (6 ounces) tomato paste

PLACE OIL in frying pan on high heat along with salt, bay leaf, garlic, hot pepper sauce, and Magic seasoning. As soon as garlic is brown, reduce heat to medium, add shrimp and remaining ingredients. Cook 2 to 3 minutes. Remove from heat and serve over pre-cooked rice.

Serves 4

Shrimp Creole Bonanza with Rice

MARTY PIERCE RUMLEY, Halifax County

"Serve shrimp creole on top of the rice," says a note from Marty. "This is a complete meal with cheese biscuits and a green salad." Before making the shrimp creole, you'll need to open the fruit cocktail, draining off, and reserving the syrup.

SHRIMP CREOLE
¼ cup (½ stick) butter
1 clove garlic, minced
1 cup onion, coarsely chopped
2/3 cup celery, sliced
1 can (28 ounces) tomatoes
2 bay leaves
½ teaspoon thyme
dash of red hot pepper sauce
1 teaspoon salt
¼ teaspoon ground pepper
1 teaspoon vinegar
¼ cup fruit cocktail syrup, see rice
    ingredients below
¼ cup cornstarch

3 cups cooked fresh shrimp or 3
    cans (4½ ounces each) dev-
    eined shrimp
½ cup green pepper strips

RICE
1 can (15 ounces) fruit cocktail,
    drained reserving the syrup,
    and divided
1 cup uncooked rice
2 cups water
1½ teaspoons salt
¼ teaspoon basil
2 tablespoons butter

TO MAKE the shrimp Creole, heat butter in skillet. Add garlic, onion, and celery; sauté until tender. Add tomatoes, bay leaves, thyme, hot sauce, salt, pepper, and vinegar. Simmer 25 to 30 minutes. Combine fruit cocktail syrup and cornstarch; stir into tomato mixture and cook until thickened. Stir in shrimp and green pepper. Heat thoroughly.

To make the rice, drain fruit cocktail, reserving ½ cup of the syrup. In a saucepan, combine ¼ cup of the syrup, rice, water, salt, and basil. Cover, bring to a boil, and simmer until rice is tender, about 25 minutes. Stir in fruit cocktail and butter, and then heat through.

Makes 6 servings

Soups
& Stews

I magine appetizing soups and pungent stews with refined flavors, abundant portions, and particular blends of textures that can only be accomplished by years of trying and improving until you just don't need to experiment any more, since you know you have it "just right." And now, smile. The very cooks who spent years perfecting these treasures have made them available to you in this chapter, the heart of this book, because soups and stews are at the core of our agricultural heritage, traditional lifestyle, and the inherited cuisine from where I grew up in eastern North Carolina.

Those of us who mark the passage of time not with calendars or watches, but by our connection to the seasons, anticipate nothing more joyfully than the ripening of the first tomato in our own vegetable gardens. Countless North Carolinians consider our most cherished local heritage to be the gifts of garden vegetables that grow so well in our soils, providing the basic ingredients for time-honored soups and stews. For us, a deep satisfaction accompanies winter's annual retreat; the return of longer, warmer days finds us beating out ancient, seasonal rhythms with spades and hoes as we prepare the ground for early spring planting. Though we take for granted the enormous variety of produce we can easily expect to thrive in our little plots, representative foods from around the world are at our fingertips and on our plates. For example, corn, tomatoes, peppers, and beans from Central and South America may be planted beside okra and black-eyed peas, which originated in Africa. Nearby, European cabbage and broccoli grow next to carrots, native to Asia. What better way to enjoy these fresh foods than by combining them into what may be the most common of all foods, soups and stews? You may not realize it, but your seemingly simple broth might be an international dish containing foods from several continents.

Versions of vegetable soup are known in almost every world culture, and ours is no exception. You can get them in restaurants, but they may not be as satisfying as the ones you probably remember having when you were growing up. The rolling, green foothills of Cleveland County are home to Terry Melton, who learned to grow a vegetable garden from her grandmother, Mammaw Pampie. They spent many happy, sunlit days there tending the family patch. Her recipe, the first of the soups, is a celebration of our food heritage as well as a special family tradition. "Go to your garden and gather," Terry tells us, "tomatoes, okra, corn, and an onion or whatever other mature ingredients you find there." Those vegetables, all by themselves, will make a nourishing and delicious soup for supper.

Where I come from, home cooking was not just an economical way to feed hungry stomachs, but used available, locally-grown resources, and hands down the tastes we grew up with. Home cooking was a creative way to make every dish suit the palates of those seated at our dinner tables. "Leftover" was not, and is not today, a culinary cuss word. Leftovers were never wasted, and became "mothers of invention" in the kitchen. They turned into lip-smacking soups or stews that could easily stretch to accommodate unexpected guests who stayed for dinner. When I have surplus vegetables now, I store them in a freezer bag until I have enough to make soup; whatever is in the bag goes into the soup pot. Maybe that's why early North Carolina manuscripts kept as personal recipe collections don't often contain recipes for soup. There was no need to write down a recipe; soup was made from a broth and whatever foods the cook had available to add to it. Here is a simple recipe that my grandmother, Alice Ward Allen, recorded in her handwritten collection during the 1940s:

3 medium sized onions cooked tender in small amount of water
3 tablespoons butter
3 cups beef stock
Place slice of toasted rye bread in each soup plate. Pour soup in and
sprinkle grated cheese on top.

While stews are basically thick soups, they have a long history in North Carolina and, surprisingly, a good deal of local culinary mystique. Food historians tell us that when the first English explorers arrived here, they found Native Americans making stews. One of the recipes in this chapter is Brunswick stew, and it is truly a food intricately connected with culinary folklore. Until I became an adult, I thought it had originated in Brunswick County, North Carolina. Then I began to hear rumors that other states claim ownership. Yes, North Carolina has a Brunswick County, but there is also a town named Brunswick in Georgia that currently displays a sign asserting its natives created Brunswick stew in 1898. Some food legends even declare that this iconic stew was first concocted in Brunswick County, Virginia, in 1828, when a hunting party set up camp in a wild area of the county. As the hunters prepared to spread out to search for game, they left a cook in camp and asked him to fix something for supper. Their story goes on to say that the cook shot some squirrels, and combined them with leftover vegetables and stale bread in a stew that simmered all day over the campfire. When the hungry hunters returned to camp, they initially laughed at the mixture, but not for long. They tried it and found it was so good that its popularity spread, and it quickly became a Southern staple. Still another version of the legend is that a politician, Dr. Creed Haskins, asked a local cook known as "Uncle Jimmy" Matthews to stir up votes by making a tasty stew to lure potential voters. Whatever its origins, North Carolinians from the mountains to the sea lovingly record recipes for it with a variety of ingredients including squirrel, beef, duck, pork, chicken, and even goat such as the two below.

BRUNSWICK STEW
Sarah A. Elliott
author of Mrs. Elliott's Housewife, Oxford, Granville County,
North Carolina, 1870

Put in your soup pot a nice fat chicken or hen (or two half grown), cover it with water salted to taste, and let it stew until it begins to look tender (the hen will have to be put on earlier than the young chickens); cut up one gallon of ripe tomatoes and season them with butter, a little onion, small cup of sugar, slice of fat bacon, pepper, and salt, as you would to stew; put them in the pot with the chicken, and one hour before you serve it, cut the grain off of twelve ears of green corn and add to it. The chicken should be cooked so it falls to pieces, and when dishing it, pick out the bones. Squirrels make a nice substitute for young chickens, and young duck will answer, or young turkey.

Jim Graham, a Rowan County native, was the Commissioner of the North Carolina Department of Agriculture from 1964 to 2000. This recipe was recorded in a publication called North Carolina Wild Game Cookery in 1977:

TAR HEEL BRUNSWICK STEW
1 large stewing chicken
1 pound veal, beef, goat, or squirrel
2 large potatoes, diced
1 large onion, peeled and diced
4 cups fresh or canned corn

4 cups lima beans

2 cans (8 ounces each) tomato sauce or canned tomatoes

salt

pepper

red hot pepper sauce

Worcestershire sauce

butter

Stew chicken and other meat together in a stock pot until chicken is ready to fall from bones. Cool and shred chicken and other meat with fingers, discarding skin and fat. Put meat back in broth, skim off excess fat and continue to simmer. Cook potatoes with onion, corn, lima beans, and tomato sauce. When potatoes are tender, combine with chicken. The mixture will be thin like soup. Simmer for several hours to thicken. Season to taste with salt, pepper, red hot pepper sauce, Worcestershire sauce, and butter.

Serves 10-12

Like the Wright brothers and Lee Smith, Brunswick stew may not actually be a native son or daughter, but whatever its origins, from one end of the state to the other we North Carolinians recognize it as being from home.

In this chapter we get vegetable chowders from the garden, chicken gumbo, chicken 'n' pastry, and Brunswick stew from the coop, and some of the most unique tastes from North Carolina's rivers, lakes, and the ocean. Becky Paul, of Davis, tells us how to make down east clam chowder and her father Claude's stewed seafood. Wilbur King is from Kinston and recounts the story of making shrimp stew on the Neuse River. John Pridgen is from Snow Hill; he shares a white fish stew the way his family has prepared it for generations. These special dishes are passed from generation to generation, because they're not only personal heirlooms, but also just plain good. Maybe that's why North Carolinians revere our cooking heritage, because it's gratifying in many ways! One of the best parts of having a common pot for a meal, as most soups and stews in this chapter are, is that they're made for sharing, perhaps by adding another can of tomatoes or some more extra corn at the last minute. When I close my eyes and think of these recipes, my stomach growls and my mouth waters for the dishes that translate my hunger into a satisfaction that doesn't just mean a full belly; they tell my soul that I'm home.

NOTES:

You can make these dishes with seafood and chicken fillets, but the resulting broth won't have the same flavor as one made with the bones left in while the broth is prepared. Bones are easily removed from broth before serving.

❧ Soups ❧

Mammaw Pampie's Garden Chowder

TERRY MELTON, Cleveland County

This recipe is a celebration of our food heritage, and a favorite summer meal when served with corn bread and biscuits.

6 to 8 very ripe tomatoes
1 to 1½ pounds okra (small pods)
6 strips bacon

6 to 10 ears of fresh sweet corn,
usually yellow
1 onion

WASH TOMATOES, put in a large aluminum pan, boil water, and pour over tomatoes. Slip skins off and chop. Wash okra; trim ends and discard, then slice. Fry bacon in bottom of large soup pot. Remove bacon but leave grease in bottom of pot. Shuck, silk, and wash corn; cut off cob, scrape cob into soup pot to make chowder thicker. Put remaining ingredients altogether in soup pot. Simmer on low to medium heat until vegetables are just cooked and chowder thickens slightly. Serve hot.

Serves 4

Miss Sadie's Vegetable Soup
with Macaroni and Beef

BARBARA NEWBOLD FLETCHER, Pasquotank County

"My mother-in-law, Sadie Chambers Fletcher, was from the Camden area and moved to Pasquotank County area when as a young girl," Barbara told me. "She lived in the Weeksville area the rest of her life. I lived next door to her for almost twenty years and learned a lot of things from her. She never made soup by any other way than what you put in when. We used to raise our own beef. So she would say to get out one or two packages of meat."

1 package soup bone or stew beef   *pot of boiling water*
   (approximately 1 pound)
1 package round steak, diced
   (approximately 1 pound)

7:30	put on the beef with salt and pepper, boil
8:30	add 2 pints of tomatoes
	continue boiling
9:45	add 3 carrots, diced
	½ pint lima beans
	½ pint green peas
	2 medium onions, diced
10:30	add 8 ounces elbow macaroni
10:45	1 pint corn
	watch carefully that it doesn't stick
	leave on stove to simmer, stir occasionally
	ready in 15 minutes

skim off top before serving

continue adding water

Serves a family

Cream of Asparagus Soup

MRS. ROBT. W. MADRY, Orange County

This recipe was recorded in the Chapel Hill Cook Book, published in 1939. In the original recipe, Asparagus is spelled with a capital "A," and that's how I've always felt about this particular vegetable too.

8 ounces fresh Asparagus

3 pints stock or water

1 medium onion, chopped

4 tablespoons butter, divided

½ cup fresh parsley, chopped

½ cup celery, chopped

2 tablespoons all-purpose flour

1 cup cream

salt and pepper, to taste

REMOVE hard part of stems from Asparagus; cook in stock or water until tender. Remove Asparagus. Set pot aside, reserving the stock. Use a small saucepan to sauté onions until just soft in 2 tablespoons of butter. Combine onions, parsley, and celery in the stock. Cook slowly over low to medium heat for 35 minutes; then strain out the vegetables, reserving the broth. Press the vegetables through a sieve (or you can use a blender) back into the broth. In the saucepan, combine 2 tablespoons of butter with the flour. Stir as you slowly heat the mixture until it becomes thick and smooth; then blend it into the broth. Cook for 10 minutes, stirring occasionally until thickened. Add the Asparagus tips, cream, salt, and pepper. Serve as soon as it's hot.

Serves 4

Cream of Broccoli Soup

MARGARET OWENS (in *Favorite Recipes from Margaret's Kitchen*), **Bladen County**

You can substitute cauliflower, spinach, zucchini, or mushrooms for the broccoli.

3 cups vegetable or chicken broth
1 cup onion, chopped
4 cups broccoli, cut into pieces
1 teaspoon tarragon vinegar
¼ teaspoon garlic powder
4 tablespoons butter or margarine

4 level tablespoons all-purpose flour
2 cups light cream or half and half
1 cup cheese, grated, optional
salt and pepper, to taste

COMBINE BROTH, onion, broccoli, vinegar, and garlic powder in 4-quart soup pot. Bring to a boil and cook for about 10 minutes. Cool slightly; then strain out the vegetables into a blender; blend until smooth, and return to soup pot. In a small skillet or saucepan, combine butter with flour. Heat slowly, stirring often, until mixture becomes thick and smooth. Gradually turn the heat up a little toward medium as you add the cream and cheese, stirring continuously. As soon as it's well blended, add it to the soup. Heat the soup, stirring until smooth, and season to taste. Serve immediately.

Serves 6 to 8

Cabbage Soup

....

MARTHA BLAINE WOODS, **Macon County**

"It's good to let it simmer a long time if possible," Martha adds. You can omit the ham if you prefer vegetarian soup.

2 cups navy beans, cooked
1 cup cabbage, coarsely chopped
1 medium onion, chopped
1 to 2 jalapeño peppers, chopped
  (optional)

salt and pepper, to taste
1 quart tomato sauce, or tomatoes,
  or tomato juice
1 cup cooked ham, diced

COMBINE ALL ingredients and cook slowly in a soup pot over low to medium heat for at least an hour.

Serves 4 to 6

Cream of Corn Soup

....

MARGARET OWENS (in *Favorite Recipes from Margaret's Kitchen*), **Bladen County**

You can substitute a 15-ounce can of cream style corn for fresh.

2 tablespoons onion, minced
3 tablespoons butter or margarine,
  melted
1 tablespoon all-purpose flour
2 cups milk

1 teaspoon sugar, optional
½ teaspoon salt
2 cups fresh corn, cut from cob

COOK ONION in butter or margarine in top of double boiler until tender. Add flour and stir until blended. Slowly add milk, stirring constantly until smooth and thickened slightly. Add sugar, salt, and corn. Mix well and cook below boiling point for 5 to 6 minutes. Adjust seasoning to taste.

Serves 4

Easy Onion Soup

SALLY CREECH, Johnston County

"Add slices of hard toast and sprinkle some grated cheese to serve," says Sally. This is also good served with a dollop of sour cream and a sprig of parsley on top.

2 cans (10.75 ounces each) beef or vegetable consommé
1 can water
1 beef bouillon cube, optional

2 cups onion rings
1 tablespoon Worcestershire sauce
2 tablespoons butter or margarine
salt and pepper, to taste

COMBINE ALL ingredients in saucepan. Simmer over medium heat until onions are done. Set off stove until cold or overnight in refrigerator. Reheat when ready to serve.

Serves 2

Potato Soup

MARIAN MOSS, Granville County

"My mama would make this for our family of four," Marian, of Bullock, told me. "She would divide it in half and add noodles to my dad's part, and cook them in another pot until done. My brother and I liked to have her homemade biscuits to eat with our soup. My church always wants me to make this along with homemade biscuits and jelly when we do the live nativity scene at Christmas."

This basic soup transforms easily into more sophisticated tastes. You might try:

- adding ½ cup of chopped broccoli or asparagus while it's cooking
- sprinkling ¼ cup of your favorite cheese on top of each bowl
- garnishing it with chopped bacon and parsley
- substituting butter for the bacon grease and adding ½ cup of half and half or cream

4 cups onion, peeled and sliced
2 tablespoons bacon grease
8 cups white potatoes, peeled and thinly sliced

salt, pepper, and Carolina Seasoning or your favorite seasoning
salt, to taste
water to cover

SAUTÉ ONIONS in bacon grease until soft. Add potatoes and season. Cook over medium heat until potatoes begin to soften. Add more water for a thinner soup.

Serves 8

Thick and Rich Baked Potato Soup

JANE LASLEY, Iredell County

"You can use skim milk for this," says Jane. "To freeze, do not add cheese and cream. When ready to use, thaw in microwave on power setting 6, then add cheese and cream and finish cooking. "You can use the skins to make baked potato skins by sprinkling them with seasoned salt, topping them with bacon bits, some chopped spring onions, and a good sprinkle of cheddar cheese, then baking uncovered at 400° until the cheese melts."

4 large Idaho (Russet) potatoes, baked in oven or microwave
½ stick (¼ cup) butter
½ teaspoon onion powder, or to taste
1 quart milk

salt and pepper, to taste
1 cup mild Cheddar cheese, grated
1 cup heavy cream
broccoli florets, cooked, optional
bacon bits, optional
spring onion, chopped, optional

SCRAPE the pulp from the potato skins, mash, and set aside. If you prefer to use a microwave oven, melt butter in large microwave-safe bowl, add onion powder, milk, potato pulp, salt, and pepper; then microwave 10 to 15 minutes on power setting 5, stirring every 2 to 3 minutes so milk won't curdle. Add cheese and cream, then microwave on power setting 5, stirring every minute or two, until cheese melts.

Otherwise, melt butter in a large, heavy saucepan. Stir in onion powder, milk, and pulp scraped from potato skins. Season with salt and pepper. Cook uncovered over low heat to prevent scorching, stirring often, about an hour. Soup should be somewhat thick. Add cheese, cream, and broccoli, mixing well. Cook over low heat, stirring constantly, until cheese melts and soup is thoroughly hot, about 5 minutes. Garnish with bacon bits and spring onion.

Serves 6 to 8

Wild Rice Soup

· ·

SARAH SAWYER ALLEN, Lenoir County

During the 1920s and 1930s, Leone Epperson, of Durham, kept her recipes in a lovingly compiled scrapbook, a combination of handwritten recipes, newspaper and magazine art, food related comments, and even poetry. It has a section entitled "Soups," and a handwritten note, "Remember that on cool days, soups will be enjoyed." Here's a good one for a cool fall day.

⅓ cup wild rice
½ teaspoon salt
1 cup water
½ stick (¼ cup) butter or margarine
1 cup celery, chopped
¾ cup onion, chopped

¼ cup all-purpose flour
4 cups milk
4 slices bacon, fried and chopped, optional
fresh parsley, washed and chopped, optional

COOK RICE with salt and water for 45 minutes in a 2-quart saucepan. Sauté butter, celery, and onion. When celery and onions are soft, sprinkle in the flour. Stir until thickened. Pour vegetable and flour mixture into the rice. Heat pan over low to medium heat. Gradually add the milk, stirring constantly. Garnish with bacon and parsley.

Makes 6 to 8 servings

Golden Cream of Squash Soup

ELAINE WHITAKER (from *Carolina Country Cooking*, 1977), Stokes County

This rich and delicious soup is to be enjoyed for a first course, not a main dish.

3 medium yellow squash, cut into
   pieces
1 can (14.5 ounces) chicken or
   vegetable broth

1 pint half and half
1 teaspoon salt, optional
1 cup cheese, grated

HEAT SQUASH in broth until boiling. Reduce heat to low; cover and simmer for 5 to 10 minutes until squash is tender. Cool the mixture, then purée in a blender at high speed until smooth. If you prefer a thicker texture, only put about half of the squash mixture in the blender. Return mixture to saucepan. Add remaining ingredients. Heat soup over medium heat until hot for about 3 minutes, but do not boil. Stir occasionally. Garnish with squash slices, if desired. Serve immediately or cover and refrigerate to reheat later.

Serves 6

Delicious Cream of Tomato Soup

MARIA WOODSON PAYNE, Rowan County

Maria calls this recipe "delicious" and it is!

4 cups peeled tomatoes

½ teaspoon baking soda

2 quarts milk

cayenne pepper, to taste

salt, to taste

1 tablespoon butter

1 sleeve (about 38) saltine

crackers, crushed

HEAT the tomatoes with the baking soda until thoroughly cooked. Pour the milk into the tomatoes, stirring well. Cook at a low boil about fifteen minutes. Turn heat down to low. Add seasonings and butter. Just before serving, thicken with crushed crackers.

Serves 8 to 12

Vegetable Beef Soup

FRED MORGAN, Randolph County

1 pound ground sirloin

1 cup onion, chopped

4 cups frozen, mixed vegetables

6 cups canned tomatoes

salt and pepper, to taste

red hot pepper sauce to taste, Fred

prefers Texas Pete

BROWN the sirloin in a skillet. Remove from heat and drain. Sauté the onions in the skillet until soft. Combine beef and onions with other ingredients in a crock pot. Cook for 8 hours on low heat.

Serves 4 to 6

Chicken and Rice Soup

MARIA WOODSON PAYNE, Rowan County

This recipe is over 100 years old. It's recorded in Maria's cookbook journal literally pinned with a straight pin to a page. It's typed in what looks like blue; however, it may be a carbon copy.

an uncooked chicken, about 5
  pounds
water to cover chicken
2 tablespoons all-purpose flour
½ cup water

1 cup rice
1 cup cream or milk
salt and pepper, to taste
a little parsley or thyme, to taste

WASH the chicken thoroughly with cold water, then place in a stockpot or Dutch oven and cover with water. Put pot on stove burner over medium heat. Once it reaches a boil, turn the burner down, and place a lid on top so that it cooks slowly for about three hours. Remove any grease that appears on the top. After the three hours, remove the chicken, skin, and bones from the pot, leaving the stock. Carefully separate the tender pieces of chicken, cut or tear them into small, bite-sized pieces, and replace them into the pot. Then bring the pot to boil slowly. Combine the flour and ½ cup water; blend until smooth, then pour into the chicken and broth. Add the rice, cream or milk, and seasonings. Let simmer another 45 minutes or until rice is cooked.

Serves 12 to 15

Chicken Gumbo Soup

JENNIE CORBITT SHAW, Vance County

From Miss Jennie's Cook Book – Southern Recipes, 1947, a book given to my mother in 1948 by her friend Clara Gatling.

3 tablespoons butter
3 tablespoons all-purpose flour
4 cups chicken broth
½ sweet red pepper, chopped
4 cups okra, chopped
1 large can (28 ounces) tomatoes
1 can (15.25 ounces) corn
2 sprigs parsley, finely chopped
1 teaspoon sugar
4 cups cooked chicken, cut into
  bit-sized pieces
salt and pepper, to taste

USE A LARGE saucepan or stockpot to combine the butter and flour. Slowly heat, stirring until thick and smooth. Add the broth, vegetables, and sugar. Heat over medium until steaming. Cook until vegetables are tender and gumbo is thick. Add the chicken and season.

Serves 8

Southern Bean Soup

JENNIE CORBITT SHAW (from *Miss Jennie's Cook Book – Southern Recipes*), Vance County

"The company of a friend seasons a meal," says Faithful Recipes for Famished Families, created by the Women of the First Presbyterian Church, Sanford, North Carolina, in 1981. This volume was a gift from a woman named Tammy who inscribed it as follows, "To the best friend I have ever had."

1 cup dried split beans plus enough water to cover them	*3 tablespoons ham or bacon drippings, or butter*
6 cups water plus more, if needed	*3 tablespoons all-purpose flour*
1 ham bone	*1/8 teaspoon pepper*
1 cup celery with leaves, chopped	*salt, to taste*
2 slices onion	

USE A LARGE saucepan or stockpot to cover the beans with cold water. Cover the pot and let stand overnight, or for at least six hours. Drain the beans, leaving them in the pot. Add the water, ham bone, celery, and onion. Let these cook gently over low heat until very tender. Then put the beans in a blender and grind until smooth or press the beans through a strainer. Add enough water to the strained beans to make five cups. Use a separate saucepan to combine the drippings or butter with the flour and pepper. Gradually heat until it becomes a thick and smooth paste. Combine this paste with the beans in the stockpot. Season with salt to taste. Serve hot. Suggested garnishes: Lemon slices and slices of hard-cooked eggs.

Serves 6

Down East Clam Chowder

BECKY PAUL, Cartaret County

"Well, when I came up here to Davis," Becky told me, "my mother-in-law was from Sea Level, and she cooked like the people here in Davis and Sea Level. Something I hadn't ever seen when I came up here was white clam chowder. Mother always cooked it like her mother did in Ocracoke; she put tomatoes in it. She made the Manhattan style. My mother-in-law,

Euletha Paul, she made the white kind. She stewed her clams, potatoes, and onions, and then she put like corn dumplings it. All was water based. They didn't use milk based on the coast. Maybe they didn't have milk or they saved the milk for something else."

4 ounces salt pork	*2 cups clam juice*
2 to 2 ½ cups of peeled, diced	*2 cups clams, minced*
white potatoes, around ½ inch	*2 cups water*
cubes are good	*salt and pepper, to taste*
½ cup onion, chopped	*soda crackers*
½ cup all-purpose flour	

FRY PORK in a soup pot over medium heat until done. Remove and drain. Pour the potatoes and onions into the remaining grease. Stir the mixture until the potatoes are done, about 10 to 15 minutes. Then sprinkle the flour over the sizzling vegetables until the entire mixture is well blended and has thickened. Gradually add the clam juice while you continue stirring. When the mixture smooths out, add the clams, and gradually add the water. Season to taste. Serve with soda crackers.

Serves 6

Easy Crab Bisque

RECIPE AUTHOR UNKNOWN, **Sampson County**

While I don't know who created and saved this rich but easy-to-make recipe, I'm grateful she did. It's from Something Old – Something New, a cookbook authored by the Women's Club of Clinton in 1975.

1 can (10.75 ounces) cream of mushroom soup

1 can (10.75 ounces) cream of asparagus soup

2 cups milk

1 cup light cream

1 can (6.5 ounces) crabmeat, drained and flaked

¼ cup dry sherry

6 pats butter

USE A 2-quart saucepan to combine the soups, milk, and cream. Heat just to boiling. Reduce heat to medium. Stir in the crabmeat. Let cook just long enough to heat thoroughly. Stir in the sherry just before serving. Remove immediately from heat and serve each bowl topped with a pat of butter.

Makes 10 ½-cup servingsv

❧ Stews ❧

Daddy's Brunswick Stew

MARTY PIERCE RUMLEY, **Halifax County**

"I remember the cold days when my father made this stew out at our farm in a black iron cooking pot over an outdoor fire and stirred it with a boat paddle," my cousin Marty told me. "Making Brunswick stew is a great project for a rainy day," she added, "and it freezes well."

2½ pounds chicken pieces
3 cans (20 ounces each) chopped tomatoes or 2 quarts of fresh tomatoes, peeled and chopped
1 cup fresh cabbage, chopped
1 large onion, chopped
1 12- or 14-ounce can of small butterbeans
3 large Russet/white potatoes, diced

¼ pound (about 5 to 6 pieces) cooked bacon slices WITH grease
1 can (16-ounces) white/shoe peg corn
½ stick (¼ cup) butter
salt and fresh ground black pepper, to taste

BOIL CHICKEN in enough water to cover it until the meat falls from the bones; this usually takes about 1¼ hours. Remove the meat and bones from the broth. Discard all the skin and bones, cut meat into large pieces, and return chicken to pot. Add tomatoes, chopped cabbage, and onion. Simmer on low to medium heat until the stew begins to cook down, usually about an hour. Add butterbeans and bacon with the grease; continue cooking down in like manner for another two to three hours until the stew reaches the desired thickness. Then add the potatoes and corn. Turn heat lower. Add butter, salt, and pepper. Continue to simmer and stir on LOW until stew reaches the desired thickness.

Makes about 3½ quarts

Chicken and Pastry

BETTY MANGUM, Robeson County

Betty is a Native American, a member of the Lumbee tribe. Her father received his doctorate for work that links the Lost Colony to the Lumbee nation. Betty is also a former schoolteacher, a County Commissioner, and a gourmet club member. "You eat first with your eyes," she told me. Betty likes for food to look simple on the plate, be beautifully prepared, and have an artistic presentation. Regarding her mother's recipe for chicken and pastry given below, she says, "Many people think pastry is a pie dough. This recipe is more like an egg noodle cooked in chicken broth." Betty says that selecting your favorite pieces of chicken is the best way to get started. Her mother's method includes using your forearms as well as your hands to work the dough into pastry and transfer it to the pot. "My mother would wash her arms thoroughly, cut the dough into strips, and place them on her forearms before walking over to the pot and dropping the pieces one by one into the broth."

2 to 3 chicken breasts, 2 to 3 pieces of dark chicken, a combination of chicken pieces and giblets or any arrangement you prefer

2 quarts of water
1 egg
2 cups self-rising flour
salt and pepper, to taste

PUT THE CHICKEN in water, and bring to a rolling boil for 5 to 10 minutes. Make a rich broth by turning down the heat and simmering until it cooks down. Pour ½ cup of broth into a mixing bowl. Add egg and stir with fork; then add 2 cups of self-rising flour. Use your hands to make dough that is soft and pliable. The dough will begin to pull away from bowl when it's ready. Let it rest by taking out of bowl. Prepare a clean linen tea towel that is only used for pastry by laying it down on a flat surface and flouring it well. Use your hands to stretch the dough out on towel. Put a little flour on top so it's not sticky and has a lightly floured surface on both sides. Roll towel with dough inside lengthwise, jelly roll fashion and begin to turn up edge of towel until you get a round cylinder of pastry. Refrigerate the dough until stiff, around 30 minutes or in freezer for less time if you're in a hurry. While the dough is cooling, finish cooking the chicken. Bring back pastry from refrigerator, and begin cutting it into noodles. Cut pastry lengths horizontally and vertically into approximately 1½-inch strips. Remove the chicken from the broth. Bring broth back to a boil. Drop noodles one by one into the boiling pot, turn down heat, and let simmer for 30 minutes. Separate the giblets, bones, and skin, and discard. Cut the meat into small pieces, and stir back into the rich pastry. Season.

Serves 4

Heart Healthy
Chicken and Pastry

MELEAH COLLIER STANLEY, **Columbus County**

"Extra pastry can be frozen," Meleah told me. "Wrap it well with wax paper in between pastry strips. Chicken breasts may be used instead of whole hen."

1 chicken, whole or in pieces with   *Water to boil chicken, about half*
    skin removed   *way in large pot*
4 chicken bouillon cubes   *salt and pepper*

BOIL THE CHICKEN in the water and bouillon on medium heat on top of the stove for about 3 hours or until done. Keep a lid on the pot. You can tell that the chicken is done in two ways: a) a meat thermometer pressed all the way to the bone will read 170º, or b) all the meat will be white all the way to the bone. When chicken is done, turn off the burner. Set aside two cups of the broth. Remove chicken from pot. Place it on a cutting board where you can slice off the meat, and cut it up into bite-sized pieces. Return the pieces to the pot. Add 2 cups of water and a touch of salt and pepper to the pot.

PASTRY
    5 cups of all-purpose flour   *2 cups of hot chicken broth*

PUT THE FLOUR in a large mixing bowl. Make a well (an indention in the center of the flour), and slowly pour in the hot chicken broth. Mix the flour and broth into a dough ball. On wax paper, sprinkle flour, place part of the dough ball on the flour, and roll out flat with a rolling pin. If it's too sticky, add more flour. If the dough is too dry, add a little more broth. Bring the pot of broth and chicken back to a slow boil. Roll dough out until very thin, about 1/16 of an inch and cut into strips. Place the strips of pastry on top of boiling water. Cook for about 12 minutes. Check for doneness. The stew should be white, not gummy. Continue cooking until it becomes white. When you're using flour, gluten is what gives a dish texture; a white color indicates that the gluten has formed and the stew is made. Mmmm! It's ready to serve!

Serves 6 to 8

Chicken and Dumplings

ELLAREE EVERHART, Davidson County

A few simple ingredients are all that are needed to make a variety of appetizing stews. For example, here's a recipe from one of my cookbooks published in 1971 by the first Presbyterian Church in Morganton, entitled *The 3 Ring Circus*:

> *ELEPHANT STEW*
> *Serves 3800*
> *1 Medium-sized elephant*
> *2 Rabbits (optional)*
> *Salt and Pepper to taste*
>
> *Cut the elephant into small bite-sized pieces. This should take about two months. Add enough brown gravy to cover, and cook for about 4 weeks at 465 degrees. If more people are expected the two rabbits may be added, but do this only if necessary as most people do not like to find hares in their stew.*

Mrs. Everhart's recipe follows:

5 pound hen, preferably fresh, not
frozen
1 tablespoon salt

DUMPLINGS
5 cups all-purpose flour
¼ teaspoon baking powder
1 teaspoon salt
1½ cups chicken broth, HOT
(you may need more if the
dough is too hard.)

PUT THE HEN in a soup pot and cover with water. Add the salt. Cook covered until tender. Save the broth, keeping it hot. Remove and discard bones, skin, and cartilage from the chicken, and set remaining meat aside. Meanwhile, make the dumplings. Sift flour, baking powder, and salt into a bowl. Mix with enough hot broth, about 1½ cups, to make dough. Roll it thin. Cut into strips 1½-inches wide by 2- to 3-inches long. Put them on wax paper as they are cut, not touching, and making layers separated by wax paper to prevent sticking. It doesn't hurt to dust a little flour onto the wax paper before layering the strips.

Heat the remaining broth to a rolling boil. Carefully drop in the dumplings one or two at a time. Add the boned chicken. Stir it just enough to keep the dumplings from sticking. Don't stir too much or it will ruin the dumplings. Boil them 3 minutes, and you're done.

Serves 6

Old-Timey Beef Stew

JAN COLLINS, Buncombe County

Recipes like this are repeated decade after decade by North Carolina cooks who contribute to local cookbooks. This one by Jan Collins is recorded in *Just Plain Cookin'*, created by the Baptist Young Women at Zion Hill Baptist Church in Leicester. No date is mentioned, but is one really necessary when the recipe is the traditional one enjoyed by many families over the years?

2 tablespoons shortening	1 teaspoon salt
2 pounds beef chuck, cut in 1½ -inch cubes	1 teaspoon sugar
	½ teaspoon paprika
2 cups water	dash of black pepper
1 teaspoon Worcestershire sauce	dash of ground allspice or cloves
1 garlic clove	6 carrots, pared & quartered
1 medium onion, sliced	4 potatoes, pared & quartered
1 to 2 bay leaves	2 cups beef gravy

HEAT THE SHORTENING until hot in a Dutch oven, then brown the meat, turning often. Add water, Worcestershire sauce, garlic, sliced onions, bay leaves, salt, sugar, paprika, pepper, allspice or cloves, carrots, and potatoes. Cover. Simmer for 1½ hours, stirring occasionally to keep from sticking. Remove bay leaf and garlic. Prepare and add 2 cups beef gravy. See the chapter on Gravies, Sauces, Marinades, and Salad Dressings for a beef gravy recipe.

Serves 6 to 8

Shrimp Stew on the Neuse River

WILBUR KING, Lenoir County

Wilbur King has deep roots in Lenoir County. His great-great grandfather, John P. Miller, was a 1st Sergeant in the Confederate 66th NC Infantry. He fought during the entire Civil War in and around Kinston, Jones County, Wilmington, Weldon, and Plymouth. He survived, returned to Kinston after the war, and fathered a son, Franklin Xavier Miller. A year later John Miller was hung and his wife shot during the anarchy that followed the war. One year-old Franklin, however, was hidden under a bed and survived.

Wilbur is known to almost everybody in the local area. That's because they've probably all eaten dinner at King's Barbecue, where he was the owner for over fifty years. The restaurant is a historical meeting place; both Confederate and Union armies crossed the property at the conclusion of the

King family at their restaurant in Kinston, NC

fighting of a major battle at nearby Wyse Fork in March of 1865. Wilbur King continues the family history in Lenoir County...his father, Frank King, opened a country store in 1937; great grandfather, R.W. was also a store operator in Kinston during the 1850s and was later the town's mayor.

Lenoir County is my home. I was weaned on the local barbecue. Traditional eastern North Carolina barbecue results from fresh local pork being very slow roasted either in a pit or on a special grill. When I was a child, pits were dug behind houses to a depth of four to six feet. The cold part of the winter was hog killing time. Hardwood logs, preferably hickory and oak, burned in the pits until they turned into very hot embers. A metal grate was placed over the coals, and half of a whole hog split down the middle was placed on the grate. Next, the entire pit was covered. A cook and helpers uncovered it over and over to refresh the fire and turn the pig during the sixteen hour roasting time; they frequently needed alcoholic refreshments to keep them warm as the process usually went all through the night. Family and friends gathered the next day, bringing side dishes such as cole slaw, potato salad, cornbread, and apple and sweet potato pies. When the pig was done and removed from the pit, the meat was coarsely chopped by hand. Barbecue sauce made from cider vinegar, salt, hot green peppers, and a little sugar or molasses added just the right zest to the meat. Many fancy portable specialty grills and cookers have been developed recently that are used to cook pigs even while being transported behind trucks, but nothing has ever beat the succulent barbecue that's served up after a cold night tending the fire with friends.

Excerpts from Wilbur King:

"My name is Wilbur King. I'm from Kinston in Lenoir County. And I want to talk about my memories of catching seafood and cooking seafood on the Neuse River when I was a kid growing up. We had what we called 'the camp' on the Neuse River down below Cherry Point, and it was a kind of ramshackle type place, just something to get out of the rain more than anything else. It was an old mobile home, and my dad built a huge porch on the front. And I had an uncle who was in the military, and he confiscated a bunch of cots from the military base.

"We'd go sometimes, and there'd be as many as twenty or twenty-five people, and everybody would sleep on cots. If it was nice, we'd take a blanket out and sleep on the beach and watch the shooting stars and that sort of thing. My dad had an old boat and a shrimp net. At dark or a little after dark two or three of the men would get on the boat and would crank the motor and go out. And you couldn't see them, but you could hear the motor going 'ummmmm.' And they were pulling that shrimp net. And after they'd pulled it for a while, they would start back into the bank, and they would yell out so that everybody'd know they were coming. So we'd all run down to the beach, and they would beach the boat up on the sand. Everybody would grab the ropes and pull the net so the seafood wouldn't escape. There was always fish and shrimp and crabs, all kinds of fish. And then we'd separate all the seafood. And then we'd go back up to the camp.

"My mother, I remember, would always make a big pan of tossed salad. Sometimes there were so many people there it would be like a washtub full and I remember how crispy and crunchy the lettuce always was. The tomatoes were always garden tomatoes, ya' know? You could make a meal on the salad.

"When we cleaned the seafood, we, I mean they, the adults, we would have fish that were fried with the French fries to go with them, and then we would have shrimp that were fried, and normally a shrimp stew which you prepare like a fish stew. Then the soft shell crabs that came out would be fried, and the hard shell crabs would be a crab stew. And I remember eating shrimp stew and crab stew until you'd just feel like you're going explode, but it's so good you just can't stop! And I remember all the adults together, my mom and dad and my uncles or whoever happened to be there, the recipe my daddy used for shrimp and fish stew is the same one I use.

"Start out by frying bacon in the bottom of the pot. That serves two purposes, of course: one, it greases the pot so the stew doesn't stick, and secondly, it certainly adds a flavor to the stew. Then he would always take his spoon, and after the bacon had fried out, would drain the grease and leave it in the pot but take the bacon out, and spread it on a paper towel. And that's what we had for hors d'oeuvres. Everybody would fight over it. And do you know I still do that? And my children, when they were at home, experienced that same thing 'cause they always waited for the bacon to come out of the pot, ya' know? And then put in water, condensed tomato soup, salt and pepper, sliced potatoes and onions, and just boil it until the potatoes and onions are tender. Then add the shrimp or the fish or eggs, cornmeal dumplings if you want.

"I remember especially, I was too lazy to eat fish stew when the fish had bones, and I was too lazy to enjoy the crab stew, because it was so hard to pick the crab meat, so the shrimp stew was always my favorite, and it still is. I prefer a shrimp stew over everything else. Crab stew is just really, really good if you're willing to take the time to break the claws and pick out the meat and that sort of thing. I think it's better than the other two really.

"But we always were able to go and back then in the mid-fifties, the seafood was so abundant as compared to now. We would just take a crab net, and walk down the bank and just scoop up the crabs, just chase them down and scoop them up, and now you have to have bait and a trap. Everything's been overfished to the point now that it's not anything like it was then. We used to just stand on the bank, take a cane pole like you go fresh water fishing with and a little hook and shrimp and just wade out into the water waist deep and just do it like that and catch croakers all day long. And now you can't find a croaker in the Neuse River to save your life, ya know? But things have certainly changed so much since then with that area being overfished and abused.

"We were always encouraged to bring all the friends we wanted to so we always had people to do things with. I have very fond memories. My father bought me a boat and motor when I was eleven years old, and I've had a boat and motor since I was eleven years old. I learned to water ski there, I smoked my first cigarette there, I drank my first beer there, I kissed my first girl there. [I] just [have] a lot of good memories of that place and that time. I remember it like it was yesterday. I was so very lucky!"

1 pound bacon
4 cans (10.75 ounces each) cream
  of tomato soup
4 cups water
salt and pepper, to taste

1 pound onions, chopped
3 pounds white potatoes, chopped
4 pounds fresh shrimp, shelled and
  cleaned

FRY OUT the bacon in the bottom of a large stockpot. Remove the bacon when crisp, leaving the grease in the pot. Drain the bacon, and eat it for an hors d'oeuvres. Add soup, water, seasoning, onions, and potatoes to the pot with the grease in it. Boil until the vegetables are done. Add the fresh, peeled shrimp, and cook another 5 to 10 minutes.

Serves 10 to 12

Coastal Plain Fish Stew

JOHN PRIDGEN, Greene County

John Robert Pridgen has spent all but three and a half years of his happy life in Greene County. Those years he was away were spent in the South Pacific during World War II, serving in the Special Services division of the infantry. His job was to carry a radio on his back, spot enemy targets, and radio back instructions to direct fire for heavy artillery to the troops. Since he grew up on a farm, he was very acquainted with logistics and never got lost. The only food he had to eat in the jungle, however, was K Rations,* "old cold beans," he says, which he found indigestible. During the invasion of Luzon in the Philippines, his weight dropped from 159 pounds to 119, and he was hospitalized in Manila for 34 days until he could eat again.

*K Rations were adopted by the military in 1942 to provide an eight-part meal for use by US troops in the field, such as Mr. Pridgen. The package contained a can of beans with a key to open it, some crackers, a powdered drink, Dentyne chewing gum, four Chesterfield cigarettes, a pack of matches, and some small chocolate squares.

When I was a child in Kinston, fish stew was a guarded male tradition that included cooking fresh fish outside in the winter over an open fire while drinking canned beer. However, John Pridgen, of Snow Hill, remembers fish stews as family events during which everyone dipped up the fragrant, spicy result of the local ponds, streams, and rivers married with the skill of the family patriarch.

Excerpts from John Pridgen:

"When I was a kid my father was the fish stew cooker for the whole section around here. Course a lot of people cook fish stew. Every time you find anybody cook fish stew, that's another fish stew. Everybody's got their own individual way they do it, what they put in it, and to their own taste. I just cook it like my daddy did. I ate his stews all my life. After a while, he got so old he couldn't handle it. He just give me his pot and said, 'it's up to you.' He always wanted to get his family together and that was one way he could do it was just say, 'I got a fish stew to eat' and they'd show up. His pot, it would feed 25, 30 people, the one he gave me. It was an old pot 'cause it was give to Mama and Daddy when they got married, 96 or 97 years ago that they got it, and he said that the legs was worn off it then 'cause it was so old when it was given to them so he give it to me, so I don't know how old it is, but I've got it now.

"Oh any kind of fish you can cook, you can make fish stew out of anything. I like rock or striped bass or drum. I prefer just plain bass out of fresh water, bass out of a pond or creek or something. I like it better than I do anything else. A lot of people like rock or drum or sheepshead or something like that, kind of a firm meat. Trout's all right but it'll break up easiest. But any kind of fish as long as you get the gravy, the rest of it's going to be okay."

"But then the main thing to get it the way you want it, is keep sampling the taste of that gravy until it gets the taste that you want, just a little bit of sting of salt and pepper, not a strong one, just a little sting, but to get the taste of the person that's cooking like he wants it to taste, then everything else will be all right. That's it!" says John.

"Daddy and I used to go fishing down on the river, Neuse River, creeks.

He carried a little pot. He would take the potatoes and the onions and the water that we needed to cook with and take all the stuff but the fish with us in the boat. And at lunch, whatever we caught, if it was a little small perch or a big fish, he'd get out there and find us some scrap wood in the low ground and start him a fire and get that grease started and I'd be cleaning some fish right there in the river. Whatever we caught, that's what we would eat. That was as fresh as you're going to get it. Just Daddy and myself and the fish stew. As the man on the radio, television, said 'it don't get no better than that.' 'Cause it's fresh meat and you're hungry, you're tired and down in a low ground. So you just get down there in the low ground and cook fish. 'Cause all those times spent with Mama and Daddy working and fishing and enjoying life like that is precious."

8 ounces of salt pork such as shoulder meat, streak of fat, streak of lean, ham, or your own favorite
1 to 2 gallons of water
2½ to 3 pounds onions, peeled, sliced
2½ to 3 pounds Irish potatoes, peeled, sliced
2½ pounds filleted fish, cut into chunks about 1 inch x 2 inches
½ cup salt
red and black pepper, to taste
1 dozen eggs
1 to 2 loaves of white bread

USE A CAST iron pot outside over a gas grill or wood fire, if you can. If not, use your favorite stockpot large enough to hold 1 to 2 gallons. Place the salt pork in the bottom of the pot, and fry out over medium heat. Add 1 to 1½ gallons water, the onions, potatoes, fish, about ½ cup of salt, a little red pepper, and a little black pepper. Bring to a rolling boil. If you need more water to cover all the food, add it. Maintain the rolling boil for approximately 1 hour. Adjust the heat accordingly so that the mixture does not burn. Do not stir; the rolling boil will move the potatoes, onions, and fish around and cook the pieces evenly. When the stew has cooked for 45 minutes, take out enough of the gravy to taste. Add salt, red, and black pepper a little bit at a time to get it to taste like you like it. Break up the dozen eggs and drop them one by one into the rolling stew. Continue cooking for 15 more minutes or until you take out a sample of onion or potato. When you can cut the onion or potato easily with a spoon, turn off the burner, as the stew is done. Serve with slices of white bread to soak up the delicious, tangy gravy.

Makes 10 to 12 servings

Catfish Stew for Six

RAYMOND FRYE AND J. D. HOWARD, **Cabarrus County**

This recipe is recorded in a 1948 cookbook entitled, The Daily Independent Cook Book 1948: A Collection of Favorite Recipes Tested and Proved in Kannapolis Area Kitchens by Some of North Carolina's Best Cooks. "Serve over rice," says a note from the cooks.

3 large onions, peeled and sliced into rings	*6 cups water*
½ stick (¼ cup) butter	*2 tablespoons Worcestershire sauce*
2 cups tomato catsup	*dash of red hot pepper sauce*
1 can (10.75 ounces) cream of tomato soup	*salt and pepper, to taste*
	1 pound catfish fillet, cut into pieces

SAUTÉ THE ONIONS in the butter using a 2-quart saucepan. When brown, add the catsup, soup, water, Worcestershire and red hot pepper sauces, salt, and pepper. Let mixture come to a boil. Add the fish. Cook for 20 more minutes.

Serves 6

Catfish Gumbo

JIM GRAHAM, Rowan County

This recipe comes from a 1977 publication of the North Carolina Department of Agriculture entitled North Carolina Game Cookery. A message on the first page from Jim Graham, then Commissioner of the NCDA, tells us that, "The purpose of this publication is to assist people of our great State in utilizing wild game and increasing consumption of Tar Heel foods such as sweet potatoes, pickles, and cornbread."

¼ cup butter

½ cup celery, chopped

½ cup onion, chopped

½ cup green pepper, chopped

2 beef bouillon cubes and 2 cups of water, or 1 can (14.5 ounces) beef broth

1 can tomatoes (14.5 ounces) or equivalent fresh tomatoes, chopped

2 cups okra, fresh or frozen, cut into bite sized pieces

2 teaspoons salt, optional

1 teaspoon cayenne pepper

¼ teaspoon thyme

2 bay leaves

1 teaspoon parsley, chopped

1 pound catfish, filleted and cut into cubes

2 cups cooked rice

MELT BUTTER in a stockpot. Sauté celery, onion, and green peppers in butter until tender. Add bouillon and water or beef broth, tomatoes, okra, and spices. Cook for approximately 30 minutes. Add catfish and rice, and simmer 15 minutes or until fish is tender.

Serves 6 to 8

Crab Meltaways and Claude's Stewed Seafood

BECKY PAUL, Cartaret County

In the spring of 2005, I attended a Community Night for Otway, in Cartaret County, at the Core Sound Waterfowl Museum and Heritage Center on Harkers Island. During these sociable events, a different Down East town is highlighted each month by a local historian accompanied, by a tasty covered dish dinner. Local folks have vibrant connections to the sea, wild ponies, and Cape Lookout Lighthouse, as well as a unique cooking style that includes water-based clam chowder, light bread, and duck stew with rutabagas. I asked Pam Morris, the Community, Collections, and Education Coordinator, if she knew some local folks who might be willing to meet with me. She recommended several excellent cooks, among them Becky Paul, from Davis, a Down East community, who welcomed me with shrimp dip and her recipe for crab meltaways below.

Crab Meltaways

½ pound crabmeat
1 jar (5 ounces) Old English
   Cheese, Becky prefers Kraft
1 stick butter, softened

2 tablespoons mayonnaise
½ teaspoon seasoning salt
½ teaspoon garlic salt
1 package of 6 English muffins

MIX CRABMEAT, cheese, butter, mayonnaise, and salts. Spread on English muffins. Freeze for at least an hour. Bake at 350° until lightly brown or tan.

Serves 6

Excerpts from Becky and Alton Paul:

Becky: My name is Rebecca Sue Brown Paul, and I'm known as Becky Paul. I live in Davis now. I've been here for forty years. I grew up in Marshallburg, which is probably six or seven miles from Davis. It's one of the Down East communities. My parents was Claude and Belle Brown, and my mother's people came from Ocracoke. And my father's people, they moved here in 1904 from Beaufort County, Pantega. My grandmother and my grandfather was from Hyde County, the town of Swan Quarter. We always had ponies. My grandfather owned an island. It's called Brown's Island. It's between Harkers Island and Marshallburg.

My father, he was a sea captain. He was [a] commercial fisherman, carried charters to the Gulf Stream. He made this when he was on the boat, and I just guessed at the ingredients, because we don't have a recipe; we just make it by eye. And he didn't like spaghetti. Well, this recipe, you have to have Franco American Spaghetti. I guess when they went on the boat they carried canned goods with them like corned beef and things to that effect. But they also cooked a lot of seafood. When they would leave here, they'd go out to Pamlico Sound. This is when he was shrimping; this isn't when he was carrying charters. He would take his potatoes and peel them, and he always diced them. Then he'd put his onion in it, and he'd cut his onion up kind of fine, and he'd fry out a streak of lean, streak of fat and put the grease in. And then he'd stew that until the potatoes kind of got tender, and then he would add the shrimp and the Franco American Spaghetti. You had to have Franco American; it won't work with that Chef Boyardee. You've got to have the Franco American! And then he said he would take the paddle fins off of crabs. He would just take the hard crabs, and break the paddle fins off, and put them in this, and cook paddle fins of crabs in with the stew. He always had cornbread with it on the boat, but later on, we always cooked light bread with it.

Claude's Stewed Seafood

4 ounces streak of lean, streak of
    fat
1 pound white potatoes, peeled
    and diced
1 large onion, peeled and diced
1 pound shrimp, uncooked and

peeled, or substitute crab or a
    combination of shrimp and
    crab
1 can (26.25 ounces) Franco
    American Spaghetti

FRY OUT the streak of lean, streak of fat in a Dutch oven or large soup pot. When crisp, remove the pork, retaining the grease. Add the potatoes and onions; sauté over medium heat until the vegetables are tender. Stir in the shrimp and crabs and the can of spaghetti. Cook until the shrimp is done all the way through.

Serves 4

Super Oyster Stew

MRS. R. H. STONE, **Mecklenburg County**

Mrs. Stone recorded her recipe for the Mulberry Home Demonstration Club in 1966. Oyster "liquor" refers to the liquid that surrounds the fresh oysters when they are packaged for shipment. "Scalded milk" means milk that's been brought to a boil, then quickly removed from the heat.

2 tablespoons all-purpose flour
1½ teaspoons salt
1/8 teaspoon pepper
2 tablespoons water
1 pint oysters with liquor

1 quart milk, scalded
½ stick (¼ cup) butter, cut into
*   pats*
paprika, if desired

COMBINE FLOUR, salt, pepper, and water in a saucepan over low to medium heat. Blend to a smooth paste. Stir in the oysters with the liquor. Simmer over low heat until oysters curl. Pour in the milk. Remove pan from heat, cover, and let stand 15 minutes. Add pats of butter gradually when you reheat the stew briefly before serving. Top with a dash of paprika.

Makes 4 servings

Corn Oyster Stew

MARGARET OWENS, Bladen County

This recipe is from a cookbook entitled, Favorite Recipes from Margaret's Kitchen. Margaret is from Kelly.

2 tablespoons butter or margarine
1 tablespoon flour
1 quart milk
1 pint oysters, cleaned and
    undrained

2 cups corn, cooked cream style
salt and pepper, to taste
parsley, chopped for garnish,
    optional

COMBINE BUTTER and flour in 4-quart saucepan. Heat slowly, stirring often, until you get a smooth, thick paste. Keep stirring over low heat while you blend in the milk. Cook until mixture comes to a boil. Add the corn and oysters with liquid. Adjust the seasoning. Cook until the oysters curl around the edges. Serve immediately, sprinkled with parsley.

Serves 6

Swan and Rutabaga Stew

VALERIE GASKILL STYRON, Cartaret County

One of North Carolina's greatest natural wonders occurs each fall when a migratory population of as many as 75,000 tundra swans arrives in eastern North Carolina. The swans mate and breed during the summer in the Arctic Circle north of Alaska and Canada, but fly southeast each year in a journey of up to 3,700 miles roundtrip. They live on or near the water in many of eastern North Carolina's lakes, ponds, rivers, and sounds. They eat aquatic foods, such as tubers and shellfish, as well as corns and grains that remain after fall harvest in local fields. If you'd like to see these magnificent birds, Mattamuskeet National Wildlife Refuge in nearby Hyde County is a perfect place to view them from November until early spring, and is easily accessible by car. For a real treat, stay until twilight when they "fly-in" to settle on Mattamuskeet Lake for the night, their bellies reflecting pink from the setting sun as they trill their wild, jubilant goodnight songs to each other. Hunting tundra swans, as well as Canadian Geese, is carefully regulated by the North Carolina Wildlife Commission and requires a permit, but if you're lucky enough to have the opportunity to try some, you can't go wrong with this recipe.

"My husband has lots of friends who hunt, and you can only kill one swan a year. And his friends that swan hunt have wives that don't cook swan; so they bring me the swan, and I cook them. I always have plenty of swan, because everybody brings me theirs. I cut it up real small because my husband likes it tender, cut like you would stew beef. I stew it in water and cook it until it's tender; then I put rutabagas on it and pastry, flour, and cornbread pastry. I normally cut up the rutabagas into small chunks ahead of time and put them in water so they won't brown. Then I put them in [the stew pot with the swan] about an hour before I plan to serve it. I like my rutabagas to have a little texture; my husband would prefer they completely cooked down. I don't measure anything [about the dumplings]. Bring the stew back to a boil before adding the cornmeal dodgers around the top. My grandmother always put the cornmeal dodgers around the side of the pot. You then have room to put the flour dumplings in the middle. This way the cornmeal and the flour dumplings don't get mixed up together. My brother says it's because my grandfather wanted them browned a little bit. The ones that were next to the pot would brown some. All I know is Grandma made it that way; so that's how we do it. We leave it to boil about 20 minutes after adding the dodgers. We don't use flat dumplings; we use round ones made from canned biscuit dough.

"I'll make dodgers out of cornmeal and some water. And I add a cup of water and cornmeal to thicken the stew. I want the texture to be sticky but not wet."

Easy Chili Beans
....

MARGUERITE HUGHEY, Buncombe County

A note in Marguerite's cookbooks says, "Jeane Knight, 1980."

1 pound lean ground beef
1 cup kidney beans
1¼ cups tomatoes, chopped
2 tablespoons onion, grated
1 can (10.75 ounces) cream of

tomato soup
2 tablespoons green pepper,
* chopped*
1 teaspoon chili powder

SAUTÉ MEAT until browned in a large saucepan over medium heat. Drain off grease. Add all other ingredients. When heated all the way through, turn down the heat to low and simmer until the mixture is the consistency you prefer.

Serves 8

Chili

TOM GRAY, Randolph County

"I remember the first time I ever cooked a pot of chili," Tom told me. "I came home from school one day to find a note on the kitchen counter from my mom, 'Tommy, there's a pound of hamburger in the fridge, a bag of chili-o mix, etc. on the counter.' Other than cooking hot dogs and hamburgers on camping trips, that was the first 'real' dish I ever prepared. My chili recipe has gone way beyond hamburger, onion, tomatoes, beans, and a bag of commercial chili seasoning since then. I hope you enjoy this recipe. It's been 'fine tuned' for about forty years now. This recipe is large enough to feed four to six folks, depending on how cold it is outside and their appetites, and depending on whatever else you're grazing on, so adjust the recipe accordingly. Serve in individual bowls, and top off with any of the following – grated cheese, sour cream, minced green onions, and cilantro. Serve with tortilla chips and pico de gallo and/or guacamole."

1 tablespoon olive oil
2 medium white onions, diced
2 to 3 garlic cloves, diced
1 pound stew beef or chicken breast, diced
2 cans (28 ounces each) peeled and whole or diced tomatoes
3 to 4 (15 oz.) cans of beans (black or kidney, or both), rinsed and drained

1 good handful cilantro, finely chopped
2 ounces unsweetened chocolate, Tom prefers Baker's
a real good squirt catsup
chili peppers (jalapeños, chipotles, etc.), to taste
salt, to taste
cinnamon, to taste

HEAT THE OIL in a large skillet. Cook the onions and garlic for several minutes until onions are translucent; then transfer them to a large stew pot. Brown the meat in the skillet, using the remnants of the oil, before transferring that to the stew pot. Add the tomatoes, beans, cilantro, chocolate, catsup, chilies, salt, and cinnamon to the stew pot, and simmer for several hours. Stir occasionally to keep it from sticking to the pot's bottom.

Serves 4 to 6

Vegetables

As I drove around North Carolina, from highlands to shore, I saw and visited farmers markets and roadside stalls on country roads and city corners, all busy with folks who hovered around colorful displays of locally-grown produce, like buzzing bees intent on finding nectar. As we prepare and cook yellow, red, green, purple, orange, white, and brown specimens, we North Carolinians become gastronomic artists who use vegetables to turn a bland-looking plate into a delectable palette of edible artwork. Vegetables are valued here not just for taste and appearance, but also because we revere the annual rituals of preparing and eating them, and the way these simple acts give us deep attachments to our regions, local histories, and family traditions. This chapter contains a profusion of vegetable dishes that will keep your palate interested every month of the year.

"In the Native American Indian culture," Ramona Big Eagle, of Mecklenburg County, explained to me, "we have what's called the three sisters: corn, beans, and squash." Ramona is a professional storyteller descended from the Tuscarora and Cherokee tribes. "Here in the eastern woodland area," she continued, "corn, beans, and squash were always planted together. Our Native American farmers would take the shoulder blade from a deer and attach a tree limb to it, and that would be a hoe. And they would till the ground to prepare the earth for planting by making hills. They would take corn seeds, kernels of corn, and put that into the ground. After the corn stalk started coming up, they'd go back and plant squash and beans, and then they would come up. The beans would go up the corn stalks as support. The leaves on the squash would keep out the weeds. They grew together. They nourished and supported each other. So they were called 'the three sisters.' Corn was one of the most important vegetables. It was a staple at every meal." Ramona tells us how to make her family's recipe for stewed corn in the following pages.

Many of the people I met said that vegetables were an essential part of their diets growing up. "In the summer we just ate vegetables from the garden for dinner, without meat," said Brenda Bowers from Valdese in Burke County. "My mother called me tomboy," Jessie Dalton, of Davidson County, told me. "I'm the oldest of seven sisters. Mother was good at everything. She cooked cabbage, collard greens, chit'lins. I used to eat onions like I did cabbage. We ate potato cakes. Lord, we grew big old Irish potatoes as big as my hand. Peel them, and boil them, mash them up. Add two tablespoons of flour and stir them up. Blend them, then fry them, and they are so good!"

"If you go away hungry, it's your own fault," Rose Speece told me when I spent a memorable Sunday at her home near Union Grove, in Iredell County, around the dinner table with Rose, her husband, Zeb Speece, and neighbors, Corinne and Alan Rash. "It used to be that when you went to visit somebody and didn't eat something, that insulted them, because that was the only thing they had to give you," Rose continued. As we feasted on fried pork and potatoes, string beans, fresh biscuits, corn, cole slaw, deviled eggs, chocolate cake with cream cheese icing, and apple-walnut pie, the air was filled with laughter and stories about the families and the area nearby where they all grew up. "If you have a lion, a bear, and a bull charging you and you only had two shots which ones would you shoot?" asked Zeb. "The bear and the lion, because you can always shoot the bull. We ate leather britches beans when I grew up," he continued. "You take your green beans and you pick 'em and string 'em and run a thread through them from wall to wall, maybe a quarter inch apart to dry them. It was a form of dehydration. Mama would take 'em down and sack 'em. You'd have to soak 'em overnight if you were going to have them the next day for lunch." I tried with little success to control myself, but every time I looked down, my plate was full. Alan said that he's from a family of eleven who lived on a 24-acre farm a mile or so away. "During the Great Depression I never remember missing a meal, but it was whatever was there," he told us. "Sometimes it would be pinto beans for a month. It was pinto beans and gravy for breakfast. We'd have pinto beans and corn bread for lunch, pinto beans and biscuits for supper. Sometimes we had dark pickles with the beans to change the taste, until my father began making sour mash whiskey to add to our income."

"To tell you the truth, I didn't know how bad the depression was until I was old enough to study it in history," Polly Barnard, an octogenarian from Hoke County, told me. "We knew we were poor. We didn't have any money, but nobody had any money. My family was never taught to value things in dollars and cents. We knew we didn't have any money, but we didn't feel poor. After I got finished with high school, I worked at Fort Bragg in Fayetteville. World War II was worse than the Depression, because you couldn't get gas. It was rationed. Sugar was rationed. Meat was rationed. So many things were rationed and even if you could get ration stamps, you couldn't always get meat if the stores didn't have any. I lived in the old Sanford House, a women's dormitory, because Fayetteville was a small town then and there were 190,000 total troops that came through the induction and field artillery training center. During the meat shortage, everything was rationed. You would take pinto beans, sage, and pepper, and some flour. You would make them in patties and fry them, and they taste very much like sausage surprisingly. That was used for breakfast food a lot of times. We called it bean sausage. Some people used that in the country. I remember Mrs. Floyd Monroe that gave us the recipe. Families were close back then and shared whatever they had."

Laura Blankenship and her grandson, Cory, who live on the Qualla Boundary, introduced me to ramps, a pungent little onion that grows wild in the mountains. They told me that up in the mountains in early spring, eating ramps is how folks stay healthy and strong all year. When the first shoots poke up, they are gathered, stewed, and eaten as a tonic so strong that children exude a heady and unpleasant smell and are sometimes turned away from school until it wears off. The Blankenships took me to a local restaurant called the "Little Princess" in Cherokee where I got a taste of the tangy onions; they went down just right as the perfect side dish for another Native American favorite, bean bread.

Laura and Cory also took me to meet Laura's mother, Lula Owl. "I was born down there on the main road (in Cherokee) the 21st day of March, 1919," Lula told me. "Rachel Reid was my grandmother. Well, she was real strict, and she went barefooted most of the time. They wore red handkerchiefs on their heads, and they wore a clean apron when they went anywhere. It wasn't just one you wore around and cooked in. They'd put a clean apron on to wear when they went out, to Cherokee or wherever.

"She cooked on the fireplace. They loved sweet potatoes, baked sweet potatoes and cornbread. You cooked your beans and stuff over a fire on a bunch of coals. They'd get a cast iron pot with a lid. Nowadays it's pinto beans. I think back then it was more October bean. You didn't go out to the store to buy stuff. You just had to depend on the mountains and the berries and stuff. You ate a lot of wild mushrooms, wild greens, sochanie, and poke and creasies and branch lettuce, bean salad that grows up in the mountains. You had to go to the mountains to get a lot of your food.

"The thing is, [when we were young] we stayed in boarding schools. They had a farm, and we had a lot of beans, I guess, pinto beans, and they'd have these big old steam pots, and they'd cook food in them. But we stayed hungry seemed like most of the time. We just ate twice a day. And if you ate potatoes at one meal, then you ate beans at another meal. You didn't have them at the same time. I can remember one time that we didn't have nothing to eat but a potato. You know you could raise your own potatoes. And you had a little old mill, you could grind your own corn to make bread or whatever.

"You call them the good old days. I tell you, the young people today I don't think could ever take what we went through even when I was raising my children. That's why we like it today. And we didn't have no bills either! I miss them days.

"Back then, you got out and worked. I started working about 1943. Well, when I started working at the hospital, I didn't know that kind of food. I had to learn Jell-O and what all that stuff was. I learned by doing, not by books. But I bought a house and land for $350 when I first started working. I had friends, good friends, and they loaned me the money and they said, 'you pay it back but don't ask where it come from.' And I paid it back. If you don't have friends, well you just can't make it. There was no welfare; there was no commodity food. I didn't depend on nothing. You worked for it. See, we raised our own beans; we didn't have to go buy them. And then we'd cook them, and put them in a big old barrel, and put salt on them and water. And put a big rock on them and, if you had roasting ears, you'd boil them, and put them in there, and you'd have pickled corn. Then you'd let that sour, and then you'd eat that in the wintertime. We still do that. You can take some home with you. Every time somebody comes, they get something," she told me as she handed me a mason jar of her corn.

Other food traditions include pairing vegetables in the same pot. When Bill Mackey, of Yadkinville, was asked her (yes, "her" – she was a tomboy) family's favorite food, she quickly answered, "beans and corn," and went on to quickly add that they were not cooked separately in her household, as it's mountain tradition that they go into the same pot. Where I come from over in the inner coastal plain, we combined boiled white potatoes with our green beans in the same pot. Green beans were so abundant then that my mother cooked them with chopped onions for variety. We also enjoyed okra cooked with tomatoes.

Another tradition is to add a little sugar to many vegetables like turnip greens, collards, and corn, because sometimes they'd be a little bitter otherwise. One cook told me that if the man of the house liked it in foods, it was added. I've seen recipes for vegetables in nineteenth century cookbooks that include a little sugar.

I was born in 1950 and don't remember a world without collards, but I never looked for a recipe either, thanks to the presence in my life of an African-American cook, Ida Mae Blount, who whipped them up regularly in our household without ever glancing at a cookbook. When my mother heard about the soul food movement in the 1960s, however, she once remarked that, "collards have really come out of the closet." I now understand that my mother's comment and our cook's talents are both representative of those times. In all the hundreds of cookbooks I've collected across the state, I've seen very few recipes for collards, probably because they were such a staple that no one ever needed to write down instructions for cooking them. However, as I traveled, I had some tasty new encounters with the rugged green leaves, including collards sandwiches made in Down East villages and in Scotland County, sometimes prepared as the focus of a fundraiser. One of the cooks who has become a close friend, Fay Kemp, grew up in Mann's Harbor. Her grandmother told her once about eating a family meal with her best friend who was serving collards. Her grandmother bit into a forkful and discovered that a worm had managed to, well, worm its way into the leaves for its own favorite meal, survive the seven washings, miss the chopping, and become part of dinner in the boiled pot of side meat and greens. Rather than reveal this fact to the other guests and ruin her friend's lunch party and reputation, she simply chomped down and swallowed her pride. The moral to this story, of course, is to make absolutely certain you wash every single leaf well, or buy your collards pre-washed with all little critters removed. My neighbor and friend, Barbara Roberson, from little Washington in Beaufort County, makes collards as well as anybody I've ever known, and shares her recipe in this chapter. Another old friend from Kinston, Liz Bryan, offers a little different take on this iconic dish; she sautés hers with olive oil. There just seem to be lots and lots of variations now.

Not everyone shares my insatiable appetite for collards, however. A cook from Elizabeth City sent me a poem that shares collards from a different perspective.

COLLARDS

I'm getting mighty tired of collards
Jest listen and I'll tell you why,
I've et so many of them things
'Til at times I thought I'd die.
Each time we have a meal
The collards are always there,
Sometimes they're cooked real done
And once in awhile they're rare.
When ma says that dinner's done
I hate to take my place,
Cause I know a pot of collards
Are going to be starin' me in the face.
I've et collards boiled
And I've et 'em fried.
I've fed some to my old dog
And he just upped and died.
It may sound kinda old,
But I ain't one to lie,
Ma pulled a new one
And made a collard pie.
Pa's got me worried
Cause he looks a little weak.

Las' night I heard him talkin'
'Bout collards in his sleep.
I've et 'em in salad
And I've et 'em baked
But I'll surely put my foot down,
If ma ever makes a collard cake.
It wouldn't be a bit surprisin'
And I believe I would scream,
If I went to the table
And ma had collard ice cream.
They're listed in the dictionary
as an edible green
And I've been eating collards
Long before I was weaned.
I've just about reached the limit,
As to what a feller can take.
I wish they'd dump every collard
Into the middle of a lake.
And when I get to Heaven,
I hope that good St. Pete
Hasn't gone and planted collards
Up and down that golden street.
'Cause if there's collards in Heaven,
There's one thing I know,
I'll catch the very first train out,
And join my friends below.

Roasted Asparagus with New Potatoes

LYNDA BEST, Duplin County

All over North Carolina, farms that once grew tobacco are developing new identities. Some grow grapes and make wine; others grow flowers. The Best family, from Warsaw in Duplin County, grows fields of fresh asparagus. From early spring until mid-summer, the family delivers the delicate spears to local families through farmers markets and produce stands. Lynda Best enjoys the fruits of her labor with several recipes, including this easy and delicious dish. "You don't have to cut asparagus," Lynda told me at her vegetable stand near Warsaw. "They naturally snap into pieces when you break them." Fresh vegetables are good and available all over the state during the produce season. This is so delicious," Lynda continues, "the tinier the potatoes are, the better this turns out."

1 pound fresh asparagus spears	1 teaspoon fresh rosemary, snipped
1¼ pound new potatoes, cut into	¼ teaspoon pepper
½-inch pieces	1/3 cup Parmesan cheese, grated
1 tablespoon olive oil	¼ cup pine nuts, toasted
¼ teaspoon salt	

PREHEAT OVEN to 450º. Snap off and discard the woody ends of the asparagus. Use a roasting pan to toss the asparagus with the potatoes and olive oil, sprinkled with salt. Spread the asparagus and potatoes in a single layer in the roasting pan. Roast for 10 to 15 minutes or until the vegetables are just tender. Remove from oven, stir in the rosemary and pepper. Sprinkle with cheese and pine nuts just before serving.

Serves 4

Bean Patties

JOY GILLESPIE, Rutherford County

"This is great made from leftover beans," Joy told me. "You can mix in homemade sausage or leftover cornbread to stretch it and give it more flavor."

2 cups cooked beans, such as pintos
1 egg, beaten
celery seed, to taste
¼ cup onion, chopped

½ cup all-purpose flour
1 cup of your favorite cheese,
grated
vegetable oil or butter for frying

MASH THE BEANS. Add egg, celery seed, onion, flour, and shredded cheese. Mix all together until fully blended. Heat oil or butter in a frying pan. Form bean mixture into small patties. Lay them into the hot pan, and fry like you would with a salmon patty.

Makes 4 servings

Boiled Cabbage

CLARA DELOACH, Northampton County

"I've been in Northampton County all my life," Clara Harris Deloach told me. "I was born in 1912. I been used to staying on a farm all my life, Jackson Gray Farm. My grandmother raised me. Her name was Anna Guthrie Harris. You raised everything on the farm except for your sugar. We worked with a hoe, because my grandmother didn't want the mule in the garden. We grew white potatoes, string beans, tomatoes, pepper, collards, [poke] sallet, cucumbers, apples, peaches, pears, plums, grape vine. The children ate the grapes. We made preserves, canned the peaches, made peach pickles. Made potato pudding, plain cake, no filling. If she didn't have no butter she used lard. She put the cucumbers in a barrel in salt until spring. She raised hogs, cows, and chickens. People used to come around selling herrings they caught near here. They put them in barrels. We had herring fish, cornbread, and milk every day, because we had two cows. We let the dairy bucket down the well in order for it to be cold for supper. It was better than milk you get now. I did love farming. We worked all day for 25 cents. We weren't never hungry. People walked down the railroad. My granddaddy gave them food, let them stay all night if they wanted to. We called them tramps and hobos. We used to kill hogs so we never had to buy no meat. My granddaddy made sausage. My grandmother made lard. My granddaddy was the son of a slave. He wouldn't talk about it much. He said we didn't want to know nothing about that. Sometimes they didn't have a change of clothes or shoes in the wintertime. Old folks went to town on Saturday. We'd go out to the chicken yard, get what we wanted, and eat all we wanted while they were gone.

"[To make the cabbage]," Clara continued, "I put the seasoning, salt, in about 2 cups of water in the pot. Wash the cabbage, let it drain. Put it in the pot. When it's done, I take it out of the water and chop it. I don't like it soft. I put a lid on it for about 20 minutes. The most important thing about cooking is the seasoning. My grandmother put salt, pepper, and butter. She thickened it with flour. That's how she made it. She had 13 children of her own and 9 grandchildren. You ate anything what was put before you. Sometimes, she cooked rabbit, coon, duck, turkey, and deer."

Easy Cabbage Cakes

BRENDA ZIMMERMAN, Rowan County

"For a different taste, add shredded carrots or zucchini," Brenda suggested. "Finished cakes refrigerate well and can be toasted on a cookie sheet to reheat."

6 cups fresh cabbage, shredded	*1½ tablespoons green onion,*
2 eggs plus 1 egg yolk	*chopped*
½ cup milk	*cilantro and Italian parsley,*
1 cup all-purpose flour	*optional*
3 tablespoons butter	*vegetable oil or margarine for pan*
½ teaspoon salt	*frying*

PARBOIL the cabbage in lightly salted water. Drain well. Soak up some of the moisture by placing leaves between paper towels. Squeeze out all the liquid. Add remaining ingredients. Mix well. Make small pancakes. Fry until cakes are golden brown.

Serves 6 to 8

Stewed Corn

RAMONA BIG EAGLE, Mecklenburg County

"Nanny and Big Polly, my grandmothers, always cooked stewed corn," Ramona told me. "It was one of my dad's favorite dishes. We would fix this constantly. It's the best stewed corn in the world. When I grew up, everybody used Carnation Milk."

1 stick (½ cup) butter, margarine, or 4 ounces fatback

6 ears of fresh corn

1 cup evaporated milk

3 tablespoons flour

1 cup water or milk, or a combination of water and milk

2 teaspoons pepper

1 teaspoon sugar

salt, to taste

"You can use a stick of butter or margarine for this," Ramona continued, "but when I was growing up, they used fatback meat. They cut it into thin strips, then fried it out until it was crispy, then took it out of that black skillet pan and let it drain, and reserved the grease for the corn. Then they'd take six shucked, washed ears of corn, cut the top of the cobs, and then [use a sharp knife to] scrape just the top half of the kernels of corn straight down, all the way around. Next you go back the second time, and cut closer to the cob. That's where your milky part comes in. That's the good stuff. You take all the rest of the ingredients, and mix it all together in a pot over medium heat, and you stir it constantly. That's the main thing, because if you don't, it will start sticking. You know it's done when the corn absorbs all the milk, and it smells good. The corn isn't hard any more, usually in about thirty minutes. Then turn it down to low."

Serves 4 to 6

Corn au Gratin

HELEN COCHRANE, Guilford County

1 can (14.75 ounces) of your
  favorite cream style yellow corn
2½ tablespoons all-purpose flour
2 tablespoons sugar, optional
2 tablespoons butter, melted
1 teaspoon salt

2 eggs, well-beaten
½ cup green pepper, chopped
¼ cup pimento, chopped
1 cup cheddar cheese cubes
¼ cup milk

PREHEAT OVEN to 350º. Grease a 1-quart baking dish. Mix all ingredients together until well blended. Pour into greased dish. Set dish into shallow pan of water in oven. Bake for 1 hour or until thick.

Serves 6

Easy Corn Pudding

DONNA MATTHEWS SAAD, Vance County

Corn grows golden each summer in this county's fields, just as it does in most of the rest of North Carolina. Originally cultivated by Native Americans in Mexico and Peru about 10,000 years ago, corn began as a tiny cob with only a few grains. As centuries passed, humans developed it into a larger and larger plant that gave its growers a reliable and delicious source of food and a more sedentary life. Archeological evidence has been found in North Carolina to suggest that corn has been grown here for at least 3500 years. This is a recipe for corn pudding that Donna remembers her grandmother making. The Matthews family still picks, shucks, packages, and freezes corn in Vance County. "Adding two eggs gives a richer, thicker result," Donna says. "Adding more sugar makes the pudding sweeter. Adding more milk makes the difference in a firmer or thinner pudding. Of course, adding more of all three will stretch the pudding to more servings if guests arrive unexpectedly. Be certain to use real butter."

1 or 2 eggs
½ to 1 cup sugar
4 tablespoons all-purpose flour
3 cups fresh corn, parboiled

a little milk, whatever kind you
have in the refrigerator
butter

PREHEAT OVEN to 350º. Combine eggs, sugar, and flour together to create a thick paste. Add the corn and a little milk. Keep adding milk until the mixture has a chowder consistency. Pour into an unbuttered, Corning Ware dish (no pun intended!). Put pats of butter all over the top. Place in oven and leave until butter melts. Take the dish out of the oven; stir the butter into the rest of the mixture until it is absorbed. Bake about an hour more when it will be have a delicious golden top.

Serves 6 to 8

Fried Mush

SUSAN FARRIS CANNELLA, Mecklenburg County

"This is what we eat in the Piedmont for breakfast," Susan told me. "My father, Charles Farris, taught me to make this."

4 cups water	1 teaspoon salt
1½ cups plain cornmeal	vegetable oil for frying

BRING WATER to boil in large saucepan. Stir in cornmeal and salt. Stir and boil mixture for 30 minutes. Remove from heat; let cool slightly, then pour into a loaf pan or dish. Refrigerate until firm. Heat oil in skillet. Slice mush to desired thickness. Fry until golden brown. Serve hot with butter.

Serves 6 to 8

Easy Glazed Carrots

DIANNE EASLEY LAMBERT, **Cabarrus County**

2 pounds carrots	3 tablespoons prepared mustard
1 teaspoon salt	¼ cup brown sugar
3 tablespoons butter	

PEEL CARROTS and trim ends. Chop into 2-inch pieces. Boil until tender, about 8 to 10 minutes. In a saucepan, heat the salt, butter, mustard, and brown sugar. Stir until syrupy. Pour over carrots when serving.

Makes 6 servings

Traditional Collards

BARBARA ROBERSON, Beaufort County

Excerpts from Barbara Roberson:

"My name is Barbara Roberson, the former Barbara Anne Everett, born and raised in Washington, North Carolina, better known as little Washington, and that's in Beaufort County in the eastern part of the state. I'm going to talk about collards. I ate collards as far back as I can remember, and my mother was an excellent cook. Nobody could cook collards like my mother. And I never really tried to cook them for my family as long as I could get them at my mother's house. But there came a time when Mother just couldn't cook them for us anymore, and I had to learn how to do it. I tried, and I would eat them, and I would be disappointed. So finally I said, 'Mother, tell me how come your collards are so much better than mine? Mine just don't taste like yours. How do you do it?' And she said, 'Barbara, you can't over season collards. They have to be seasoned right.' And by that she meant the broth that they're cooked in, or the meat, or the ham bone, or the piece of country ham, or the bacon grease. And back when I was growing up, you didn't worry about bacon grease. I mean we saved bacon grease to fry cornbread, and to fry fish, and to fry whatever you wanted to fry. And, of course, it was delicious. We don't do that so much anymore, but anyhow, finally I can honestly say I think they're just as good as my mother's or almost as good.

"First of all you've got to have some good collards. If you're going to buy them in the grocery store, then I'd say buy the little tender ones. It's better if you can buy them from somebody who has a collard patch. And that's what I have done for the past few years when I lived in Garner. There was a man my husband had discovered and knew, and he had this collard patch. He had learned to cook collards from his daddy, so this went way back. He had raised collards for many, many years so we would get his collards. My husband would go get them; I would go to the store, and get three or four ham hocks depending on how many collards you're going to cook. And usually I had a ham bone in the freezer or some broth from a honey-baked ham that I had. We would eat the ham, and save the bone, then I would cook the bone and get this delicious broth from it. You could mix those different meats. If you had a piece of country ham, you could throw that in there. But you cook the ham hock, if you just had ham hock that's okay too, and you cook it until it just falls apart, just falls off the bone. And then you want to take the skin out and the fat. There's some lean meat in there that is pretty darn good, so I would save that, and mix that in with the collards when they're done.

"So you've got your broth [also called pot liquor], you may have to add a little water to it, the broth doesn't have to cover all of the collards, because when you put the raw collards in there, and once they start wilting, they cook down, you know they just get smaller and smaller. So you want to start out with a pretty good pile. What I do is take each leaf and look at it back and front for insects. And I do that no matter how many collards I have, I look at every leaf, back and front, and I know that when I bite into those cooked collards, they're clean. So then I take several collard leaves and wash them well, and then take a knife and just cut them up. Go ahead and cut them before you cook them. I didn't used to do that, slice them up, but I found it works real well. They fit in the pot better. So I just slice them up and press them down into the pot liquor.

"You may want to put just a teaspoon, no more than that, of sugar. Sometimes collards can be a little bitter. You may want to try them, but it probably wouldn't hurt to put a little bit of sugar in there. And you'll probably have to salt them some more, and add some pepper.

"You just cook the collards, and keep checking them until you stick your fork in them, and they're nice and tender. When you think they're done, you just get a little saucer or a little bowl, and take you out a nice serving, and cut it up some more if it needs it, and taste of it. If it needs a little more seasoning, if you've got some bacon grease, and you want to put a tablespoon in there, it gives the collards a shiny look. And, oh man! They'll just make your mouth water!

"When you get them tasting just like you want them to taste, and they're nice and tender, just take them up with a slotted spoon, drain the pot liquor off of them, then you can serve them plain just like they are, or a lot of people like hot pepper vinegar on them. Some people use different kinds of relishes. But I just like the plain old collards myself. If they're seasoned right, they don't need anything else on them.

"Another thing that Mother did, and I did for a long time for my children, I have four children, and they all love collards, and their husbands love collards, and even the two sons-in-law that are Yankees love collards. You know, they've got to be pretty good for a Yankee to love collards! We would put potatoes in there and sort of put them towards the last half of the cooking.

"And the last fifteen minutes if you like them, something my mother always did and we liked, was [add] cornmeal dumplings. It's nothing in the world but cornmeal and water and salt. And you want to use hot water, and you want to let it set for a little while, just a few minutes, because it'll thicken. And then you want it just the right consistency to kind of roll it up in your hand like you're making a biscuit, and then patting it out, not too thick. The small ones are nice, I think. And drop them carefully on top of the collards, and let them cook the last fifteen minutes of the cooking time. So you just take those out, and you can put those in your pot liquor after you cook your collards if you want to, or you can just lay them on top of your collards, and let them cook. You take them out first, and then take your collards. Of course, people do things their own way and different ways and whatever works for you.

"Let me give you one more little hint that I especially like. I like the leftover dumplings, because after they're cold the next day, you take those dumplings and slice them like you're slicing a hamburger bun, and you put them in a frying pan. I would have used bacon grease years ago, but today I would use a little cooking oil, and brown it, crisp, like corn bread. If you have any leftover collards, and you've got those fried leftover dumplings, you just can't beat it! It's just so good, I just can't tell you how good it is. My mouth is just watering sitting here thinking of it. But that's how I cook collards. I hope you'll try them, and I hope you'll enjoy them."

Traditionally, collards are best when picked after the first frost.

3 or 4 ham hocks
broth from ham (saved from previous meals), if you have it
½ - 1 teaspoon sugar, optional
salt and pepper, to taste
cornmeal dumplings, if desired!
Good, fresh, collards – smaller, tender ones are best. Collards are part of the cabbage family and grow in a head. For a full pot that will feed up to four to six people, you'll need the equivalent of a full head of collards. This may seem like a lot but they are just leaves and reduce down quickly when cooked.

COOK THE HAM hocks by slow boiling in saved broth and/or water, enough to cover, until the meat falls off the bone. Remove and discard the bones and fat, but leave some of the meat in the broth...it should have cooked down into small pieces. Wash each collard leaf carefully, back and front. Chop the leaves into pieces, perhaps as small as 1 to 2 inches depending on personal preference, but do not mince them. The stalks will be firmer than the leaves and may be left in or taken out. Leaving them in will give the final cooked dish a firmer texture. If you do leave them in, chop stalks well into more or less 1-inch pieces. Heat the remaining broth, then add the collards. Add enough water to the broth to reach the level of the leaves, but not cover them. Simmer the collards over medium heat until they cook down and become tender. At this point, the pot will produce the strong, smoky aroma that makes these greens famous. When a fork goes easily through the stalk pieces, they're done. Taste them. If you find them a little bitter, you can add a teaspoon or less of sugar. Salt and pepper to taste, and you can add a teaspoon of bacon grease for extra seasoning and to give the dish an appealing shine. To serve, drain with a slotted spoon, eat plain, or with hot pepper vinegar or chow chow. Sop "pot liquor" with cornmeal dumplings…

CORNMEAL DUMPLINGS

about 1 cup plain cornmeal   *½ to ¾ cup hot water, to make*
about ¾ teaspoon salt   *corn meal firm but not mushy*

Mix cornmeal, salt, and water to biscuit dough consistency. Form small balls in the palm of your hand, then press each down to make a small, flat dumpling. Place the dumplings on top of collards or in pot liquor for ten or so minutes. Leftover dumplings can be fried in bacon grease and served with leftover collards. Serves 6.

Chapel Hill Collards

LIZ BRYAN, Orange County

Liz uses Soul Seasoning to flavor her collards. It's a delicious blend of salt, paprika, garlic, onion, curry powder, black pepper, celery, chili powder, red pepper, parsley, and cayenne pepper. Many local stores carry it. "I get mine at the Dollar Store," she told me. "There's nothing formally written down, but here's how I cook 'em. You'll need a large bunch as they cook down. It's very important to pour off the liquid after cooking, as collards get bitter if left stewing in their juices. My friend, Rosemary, taught me to appreciate collards with a baked sweet potato. My family enjoys healthy eating!"

1 large bunch fresh collards
Soul Seasoning, to taste

approximately ½ cup olive oil, depending on how much you like

WASH THE COLLARDS thoroughly in a sink full of water. Pick up as many leaves as you feel comfortable stacking together. Trim the stems so you have fresh ends. Roll up the leaves starting on the long side, for easier handling, and chop starting at the stem end. Place the chopped pieces in large saucepan with a lid, adding about 2 inches of water to the bottom of the pot. Sprinkle first with Soul Seasoning, then liberally with olive oil. Bring pot to a boil, then reduce heat to a low simmer. Cover, and cook for an hour. Remove from heat and pour off the liquid, but reserve it. "You now have some fine collards which will also taste good reheated, and you have some pot liquor to use for making soup," Liz concludes.

Serves 8 to 10

Collards and Cabbage with Salt Pork

TIMI DOYLE, Wake County

> 3 tablespoons apple cider vinegar
> 6 to 7 ounces salted pork
> crushed red pepper, to taste
>
> 1 bunch fresh collards
> 1 head cabbage

HEAT WATER in large soup or stockpot. Add the vinegar, salted pork, and red pepper. Simmer while you get the collards and cabbage ready. Wash collards well, then chop. Be sure to cut the cabbage up, but not into tiny pieces. Large pieces are better as it will fall apart while cooking. Add collards and cabbage to the pot, then bring to a boil. Reduce heat to simmer. "I like to cook it for at least 1 hour or longer," says Timi, "till the taste tells you it's the way you want it."

Serves 8 to 10

Collards Sandwiches

KAREN GOINS, Scotland County

"I'm a native of Laurinburg in Scotland County," Karen told me. "A lot of the churches have collards sandwiches sales, and it's a big seller for the churches. Everyone seems to buy them. You fix the cornbread separate. You fry the cornbread. Autry is the best if you can get it, plain yellow cornmeal. Salt and pepper, you put self-rising flour, about ¼ cup to 1 cup of cornmeal, and I use hot water to mix it up. Mixing it with hot water does best. I add water, and stir it until the batter is thick, but not too thick, and certainly not runny. You don't want it so thin that when it's cooked, you can't pick it up, and bite it. It's all in the feel. You just have to have a feel for when the cornmeal batter is thick enough before you fry it. An iron skillet is probably the best, but I use a club aluminum frying pan. As a matter of fact I have my grandmother's old iron skillet, but it doesn't have a handle on it. I used to use it for cornbread, and I fried chicken in that same pan, because it cooks good. I use vegetable oil to fry the cornbread, but for the collards, you have to have either fatback or pork seasoning. You pour the cornbread batter into the pan a little thicker than a pancake. You want the patties to be kind of large, because you're going to put your collards in them. You know when it's done, because it's browned all over, crisp, and golden brown. You don't want it to be soft in the middle. After you fix your collards (see recipes in this chapter), then we take the collards, and put a flat piece of cornbread, collards, then another piece of cornbread. You give them a piece of fried fat back with them and some hot pepper. And it is terrific!"

Fried Okra

TIMI DOYLE, Wake County

In 1812, a family named House moved from England to America. They had a mill stone shipped to Wilmington, then barged up the Cape Fear River to Newton-Grove. The House Mill ground cornmeal and prospered. In 1967 it merged with Autry Brothers Mill, another local business. In March of 1865, the Confederacy mounted its largest offensive of the war in North Carolina in nearby Bentonville. I've heard food gossip that House Mills supplied both armies until someone shot their delivery mule for food. After being in business for over 200 years, the company has expanded its product line to include the chicken breader used for Timi's recipe. "Use more egg and water if you have lots of okra," says Timi. "I grow my own okra. It's easy!"

shortening for frying, Timi prefers Crisco

1 egg

1½ teaspoons water

1 pound fresh okra

1 cup chicken breader, Timi prefers House-Autry

onion salt, to taste

HEAT SHORTENING in large skillet 1½-inches deep over medium heat. Beat the egg and water together. Slice the stem ends off the okra, rinse, and add to the beaten egg mixture. Stir or toss until all okra is moist. Coat the okra well with the breader. Fry okra in heated oil. Don't worry if you don't get it all separated. Cook in small batches until golden. Drain on paper towels and sprinkle with onion salt, a must for great okra.

Serves 4

French Fried Onion Rings

FOY ALLEN EDELMAN, Lenoir County

If you like tart onion rings, use yellow – we used to call these "Bermuda" – onions. For a sweeter, juicier flavor, use a sweet onion like a Vidalia. There are two tricks to making great onion rings. First, make certain the shortening is hot before adding the batter-covered onion rings. Otherwise, they'll come out of the grease soggy. You can test this by sprinkling a tiny bit of water in the grease after it's hot. If the water pops and crackles, it's ready to fry your rings. Second, fry a single layer at a time.

2 large onions 1¾ cups milk, divided	1 teaspoon salt
½ cup plain cornmeal and ½ cup all-purpose flour, or you can use 1 cup of either	¼ teaspoon pepper
	1 egg
	vegetable shortening for frying, I prefer Crisco

PEEL THE ONIONS, then cut into ¼-inch slices. Pour a cup of the milk into a large bowl. Separate the onion slices into individual rings, then put them into the bowl of milk. Let them stand for at least 15 minutes, moving them around so that all the slices are doused with milk. Make a batter by combining the cornmeal, flour, salt, and pepper. Heat enough shortening in a frying pan to make about an inch when melted. Make sure the shortening is hot before coating the onion rings with batter and dropping them into the fat. Fry one layer at a time. Turn them when they begin to brown. When browned on both sides, drain well. These are best served hot.

Serves 4

Easy Parsnips

KATHERINE SAWYER WARD, Bertie County

"They look like large white carrots," says Katherine. "My Thanksgiving dinner wouldn't be complete without turkey, dressing, gravy, ham, collards, snap beans, corn, butter beans, parsnips, and cranberry sauce."

8 parsnips	butter, melted
salt and pepper, to taste	fresh parsley, chopped, optional

PEEL PARSNIPS like you do carrots. Cut down the middle, then into uniformly sized pieces so that they cook evenly. Leave smaller end uncut. Put them in a saucepan and cover them with water. Boil until tender, about 10 to 15 minutes. Test with a fork. When tender, they're done. Season, and serve warm with melted butter and chopped parsley.

Serves 6 to 8

Black-eyed Peas

CAROLYN GOFF, Harnett County

"I don't mind telling you the secret of my black-eyed peas," Carolyn told me. "It's a tad bit of celery and parsley."

4 ounces salt pork, diced or sliced	*1 stalk celery with leaves, chopped*
2 cups dried black-eyed peas	*1 teaspoon chopped parsley*
4 cups water	*salt and pepper, to taste*

FRY THE PORK lightly in a Dutch oven or other large pot. When the meat begins to brown, add the peas, water, celery, and parsley. Bring to a boil; then lower the heat and simmer for 2 hours. Then taste them and season with salt and pepper.

Serves 8

Easy Traditional Field Peas

BRENDA HOWELL, Wayne County

Fresh picked field peas are delicious, nutritious, and easy to obtain and prepare. Some people call these "cowpeas." Food historians say they originated in Asia, but came to our part of the world from Africa during the early days of colonial America. Like many other non-native foods, North Carolinians have claimed them as their own.

1 ham hock   *½ teaspoon salt*
4 cups fresh field peas

COVER HAM HOCK with water in a 2-quart saucepan. Bring to a boil, then turn heat down and simmer until the meat is tender. Stir in peas and salt; add water just to the level of the peas. Continue simmering until peas are tender.

Serves 8

French Fried Pickles

LYNN WILLIAMS, Wayne County

Lynn Williams works at the corner of Cucumber and Vine in Mount Olive, North Carolina. Her employer, Mount Olive Pickle Company, started into business in 1926 when investors purchased one acre of land for $1000. During the first year, the entire operation was completed by hand. Workers carried brined cucumbers from barrels to a nearby table where they put them into jars and then poured syrup over them from old coffee cans. Today, Mount Olive Pickle Company is a modern company, and the country's largest privately held pickle company. It packs over 110 million jars of pickles annually.

vegetable oil

1 egg

3 tablespoons milk

1 tablespoon pickle liquid (dill or sweet) or banana pepper rings

1/3 cup dry pancake mix

1 cup pickle slices (dill or sweet cucumber), well drained

HEAT 1 INCH of cooking oil in a cast iron or electric skillet to 360° on deep-fat thermometer. Slightly beat egg in small mixing bowl; stir in milk and pickle liquid. Add pancake mix; stir until smooth. Dip pickle slices, one at a time, into batter. Fry in oil 1 to 2 minutes until lightly browned. Remove with slotted spoon and drain on paper towels. Serve immediately.

Makes about 2½ dozen

Oregano Pinto Beans

MRS. NED BURGESS, Suburban Home Demonstration Club

This recipe was recorded in 1966 in foods we remember, a cookbook compiled by the Mecklenburg County Home Demonstration Club.

1 cup pinto beans, dried

4 ounces salt pork, cut into pieces

1½ cloves garlic, finely chopped

½ teaspoon oregano

dash of red hot pepper sauce

½ teaspoon salt

This recipe takes 4 hours. Be sure to add water as needed to keep beans moist and tender. Place beans in a 2-quart saucepan just covered with water. Bring to a boil; then simmer for 1 hour. Add salt pork, then simmer for another hour. Add garlic and simmer for another hour. Add oregano and red hot pepper sauce; simmer another hour. Add salt and serve.

Makes 6 ½-cup servings

Easy Favorite Potatoes

BRENDA ZIMMERMAN, KELAINE ZIMMERMAN HAAS, Rowan County

"This is a great vegetable to serve for company," Brenda told me. "It's easy to make and looks nice on a plate. Once cooled, it's a good finger food for children. You might want to vary the spices you use depending upon the main course."

4 baking potatoes
½ stick (¼ cup) margarine or butter
salt, to taste

generous sprinkling of your favorite spices, Brenda prefers garlic powder, oregano, curry powder, and seasoning salts

PREHEAT OVEN to 400°. Wash and scrub potatoes. Cut in half along the length of the potato. Use a paring knife to score the potato halves with crosshatched lines about ½-inch apart. Use a cookie sheet to melt the margarine. When melted, remove from oven and sprinkle generously with spices. Place potato halves, skin side up, over melted butter with spices. Bake until the backs are easily pierced with a fork and the scored sides are brown and crispy.

Makes 8 halves

Easy Potato Puffs

FRANCES ROBINSON, **Buncombe County**

vegetable oil for frying
2 cups mashed potatoes
2 eggs, beaten

½ cup self-rising flour
milk or cream
salt and pepper, to taste

HEAT A PAN of oil on stovetop. Mix potatoes, eggs, and flour in a bowl. Add enough milk or cream to make the mixture the same texture as mashed potatoes. Drop by spoonful into hot oil and fry until brown. Season, and serve immediately.

Serves 4

Irish Potatoes with Cheese

GLENNIE BEASLEY, **Chatham County**

"This is good in place of potato salad," Glennie told me. "I got this recipe from a friend of mine, Louise Womble."

4 medium white potatoes, peeled
1 medium onion, chopped
1 stick (½ cup) margarine or
    butter, divided
1 cup breadcrumbs

garlic powder and onion powder,
    to taste
1 pound Velveeta cheese, shredded
fresh sprigs of parsley, chopped,
    optional

PREHEAT OVEN to 350°. Grease a 2-quart baking dish. Boil potatoes just like you boil them for potato salad. Cut them into cubes. Sauté the onion in ½ stick butter until browned. Add the breadcrumbs to the onion, and sauté them together. Add the onion mixture to the potatoes; season with garlic and onion powder. Layer the potatoes and onions with the cheese until all is used. Sprinkle parsley on top. It's already cooked, but you put it in the oven until all the cheese is melted, about 15 minutes.

Serves 6 to 8

Easy Baked Pumpkin

BETTY OXENDINE MANGUM, Robeson County

> *1 small baking pumpkin*
> *2 tablespoons honey*
> *2 tablespoons apple cider*
>
> *2 tablespoons melted butter or*
> *margarine*

PREHEAT OVEN to 350°. Wash the pumpkin well; place on a pie pan or biscuit sheet. Bake for 1½ hours. Remove from oven, and cool until you can handle it. Then cut a hole in the top of the pumpkin around the stem, about 3 to 4 inches in diameter. Scoop out the pulp and separate it from the seeds, reserving the pulp. Mix the pulp with the honey, cider, and butter. Baste the mixture over the flesh of the pumpkin. Replace top, return moderate oven, and continue to bake for 35 to 40 minutes longer, basting occasionally. Serve whole, scooping out the individual portions at the table, or cut into wedges as you would a melon. Ladle a little of the cider mixture over each serving.

Serves 6 to 8

Easy Brown Rice

FOY ALLEN EDELMAN, Lenoir County

2 tablespoons butter
1 small onion, chopped
1½ cups long grain rice, uncooked
2¾ cups water

1 can (10.5 ounces) beef
   consommé
dash of salt

HEAT BUTTER in 2-quart saucepan. Add onion, and sauté gently until onion pieces turn yellow. Add rice and salt, stir continuously until all is golden brown. Add the consommé and water, cover pot tightly, and simmer for 20 minutes without lifting the lid. Then stir lightly with a fork. If you prefer a drier rice, cook a few extra minutes uncovered.

Serves 8

Rutabagas

BILLIE STROUD, Duplin County

Excerpts from Billie Stroud:

"I grew up in Duplin County out from Chinquapin on a farm. The washhouse is still there with the pots where they did the hog killings and pulled the lard out. This is just good country cooking. Some weekends we cook, wash dishes, and start cooking again. I learned to cook rutabagas from my mother; she was a Brinson from Cedar Fork. I think of them as fall vegetables, but you can get them all year. They're traditional food. When my Aunt Doris died, several people brought rutabagas over.

"I boil water in a large saucepan. Then I add some kind of cured meat, salt and pepper; you can add a ham bone, a piece of country ham, or even bacon drippings. It depends on how much flavor you want. If you want to reduce the amount of fat, you could use some type of bouillon instead. Then I peel my rutabagas and cut them into pieces like I would a white potato. When you get ready to peel them, you need a real sharp knife and sometimes a real strong grip, because they're often covered with wax, and they're a lot harder than potatoes. Sometimes you can find unwaxed rutabagas at healthy style grocery stores like Whole Foods or Fresh Market. I peel them first before I chop them so there's no wax left when I cook them. If you're in a hurry, you can cut them into really small pieces. If I'm not going to cook them right away, I cover them with water. I add a tiny, I mean tiny, bit of sugar, a pinch, even a few grains. It makes all the difference in the world to the taste. I boil mine until they're tender enough to mash, then I remove them from the broth, put them in a bowl, and coarsely chop them. They look like lumpy mashed potatoes. If they're too dry, you can add a little of the broth to them. When they're cooked, they turn a beautiful rich burnt-orange color.

"I like to have rutabagas with pork tenderloin for dinner. This is a quick, quick meal; it doesn't even take 15 minutes to fry the tenderloin. I cut up my pork, and fry it in a cast iron skillet with oil like I would chicken. I let it brown on one side, then turn it once. If you turn them too quick, they stick. I know it's done when the sizzling noise suddenly quiets down and stops popping. That means the meat is cooked all the way through. Then I take the pieces out and drain them. I add flour to the remaining grease drippings, stir it until it's smooth. I usually serve it over rice. Green beans, butter beans. I have had it with rice for breakfast."

Baked Herbed Spinach

SARAH SAWYER ALLEN, Lenoir County

My mother's notes attribute this recipe to Ann Cooper, of Windsor. It was part of a luncheon menu at St. Thomas Episcopal Church, built in 1839. You can substitute an equal amount of cooked fresh spinach for the frozen but be careful to wash it well in salt water as fresh spinach often has grit in it. This dish can be made ahead, and cooked the day you serve it.

½ cup onion, finely chopped
1 clove garlic, minced
½ stick (¼ cup) butter or
    margarine
2 packages (10 ounces each) frozen
    spinach, thawed

½ cup cream
½ cup milk
¼ cup breadcrumbs
1 teaspoon marjoram
salt and pepper, to taste
½ cup Parmesan cheese, grated

PREHEAT OVEN to 350°. Grease a 2-quart casserole. Sauté onion and garlic in butter until tender. Combine onion with spinach, cream, milk, breadcrumbs, marjoram, salt, and pepper. Pour into prepared dish. Sprinkle with Parmesan cheese. Bake for 30 minutes.

Serves 8

Squash Patties

....

WANDA BROOKS, Stanly County

3 cups squash, grated and raw   1 teaspoon sugar
1 medium onion, chopped   ¼ teaspoon black pepper
¼ cup milk   ½ teaspoon salt
1 egg, beaten   1 cup grated cheese
¼ cup vegetable oil   Crisco or vegetable oil for frying.
1 cup all-purpose flour

COMBINE ALL INGREDIENTS in medium sized bowl. Mix well. Drop by tablespoon onto hot greased skillet. Fry until golden brown, turning only once. Drain on paper towels. Serve immediately.

Makes 2 dozen

Easy Succotash

....

BETTY OXENDINE MANGUM, Robeson County

This is outstanding in the early summer when you can get fresh lima beans. If you use canned lima beans and corn, be sure to drain them before adding to the onions and green peppers.

6 strips bacon   2 cups baby lima beans
1 onion, coarsely chopped   2 cups corn
¼ cup green pepper, chopped   salt and pepper, to taste

SLOWLY FRY out the bacon until crisp. Remove the bacon, leaving the hot drippings in the pan, then sauté the onion and green pepper. When the onion is golden brown, add lima beans and corn. Cover and simmer for 10 to 15 minutes. Season and enjoy.

Serves 8

Easy Sweet Potato Cakes

BETTY OXENDINE MANGUM, Robeson County

Farmers in the Inner Coastal Plain make North Carolina the biggest producer of sweet potatoes in the country providing a vegetable with an enticing flavor, low cost, and high nutritional value. You can experiment with varieties that have a range of delicious tastes and textures. Some have robust flavors, sweet, and smooth, like the Beauregard, while others, like the White Delight, are chewy and have an intriguingly subtle taste. The seemingly endless ways to prepare them – bake, roast, stew, boil, fry, sauté, and mash them – make this vegetable extremely popular. This recipe is a great way to enjoy them. "Be sure to serve these hot with butter and honey," says Betty.

4 large sweet potatoes　　　*dash of black pepper*
3 eggs　　　　　　　　　　　*vegetable oil for frying*
1½ teaspoons salt

PARBOIL THE POTATOES until tender; peel, and mash them. Mix in the eggs, salt, and pepper. Heat the oil on a griddle until a drop of water sizzles; drop the potato batter from a large spoon, and brown on both sides. As you turn the pancakes, flatten them with a spatula slightly. Add more to the griddle as needed. This recipe will make about 15 cakes that are about 3 inches in diameter.

Serves 10 to 12

Fried Sweet Potatoes

∙∙

NANCY MEDFORD HYATT, Haywood County

"I am Nancy Medford Hyatt from Haywood County. I was born in this county and have spent my whole life here. I learned to cook some things from my mother, my grandmother, and my great-grandmother. Many of my recipes have never been written down, like fried sweet potatoes. All you do is take your sweet potatoes, peel them, then cut them into rounds about 3 inches in diameter and ½ inch thick. Sauté them in a skillet over medium heat with butter until soft enough to eat."

Sweet Potato and Greens Stir Fry

∙∙

KATE MCKINNEY MADDALENA, Wake County

"I'm a native of Raleigh and graduate of UNC-Greensboro and North Carolina State University. Southern food is my culinary 'mother tongue,' but my personal 'dialects' tend to the East – I love fresh Lebanese tastes: lemon juice, olives, parsley, chickpeas, eggplant, and Chinese-inspired stir-fry. The cool thing about stir-fry is the fact that you can add whatever you've got. These ingredients are absolutely up for experimentation. My recipe is a marriage of these influences – my grandmother loved sweet potatoes, but she would never cook them this way!!! This dish may be eaten straight from the wok, rolled in a tortilla, or served over noodles or rice. It was created in the spirit of inventiveness and BEGS to be tampered with..."

olive oil

2 large sweet potatoes, cut in flat spears

4 cloves of garlic, minced

½ large red onion, chopped

rice wine vinegar

½ head red cabbage, cut to strips

6 leaves collard greens or kale, rinsed and chopped

2 eggs

soy or teriyaki sauce

red hot pepper sauce and/or red pepper flakes, optional

COAT THE BOTTOM of a wok or a LARGE frying pan with olive oil and add the potatoes. Cover to cook completely, but turn them occasionally. When they begin to soften, reduce heat, and add garlic and onion. Add a dash of rice wine vinegar to seal taste, then the greens and cabbage. Cover to allow leaves to cook down, turning often. Make a space at the bottom of the wok for the eggs, crack them in and let them cook, breaking the yolks. As the eggs brown, stir them gently into the rest of the mixture. Lastly, add a generous shot of soy sauce, and allow it to cook down. Red hot pepper sauce or red pepper flakes may be added for spicier palettes.

Serves 2 to 4

Easy Tomato Puddin'

EDNA HOLLEY, Bertie County

1 large can tomatoes

1 - 1½ cups sugar

2 slices bread, crumbled

salt and pepper, to taste

COMBINE ALL INGREDIENTS in saucepan on top of stove. Heat slowly, stirring frequently, because it will stick easily. When blended well, turn down burner, and simmer for 20 minutes.

Serves 4 to 6

Mary Charles Pawlikowski, Edna Holley, and Betsy Ward Price

Tomato Pie

CAROLYN GOFF, Harnett County

You can substitute canned tomatoes for this pie if you drain them well.

1 unbaked pie shell

5 to 6 fresh, ripe tomatoes, washed, skinned, cored, and quartered

½ cup mayonnaise

½ cup Parmesan cheese

½ cup mozzarella cheese

PREHEAT OVEN to 375°. Pierce the bottom of the pie shell several times with a fork; bake for 5 minutes. Remove the pie shell; reduce oven temperature to 350°. Arrange tomatoes evenly in pie shell until it's filled. Combine the mayonnaise with the Parmesan cheese; then spread on top of the tomatoes. Sprinkle top with mozzarella cheese. Bake for 30 minutes, or until the cheese is completely melted, and the tomatoes are hot and bubbly.

Serves 4 to 6

Salads
& Fruit

I'm definitely a child of the sunny South where the growing season is long and harvests are plentiful. To me, a day without salad is a day without sunshine. I'm one of few people I know who can, and often do, eat salad three times a day. While I didn't grow up on a farm, I grew up in a small town that was surrounded by beautiful, plentiful farms that stocked local grocery stores like the Piggly Wiggly and IGA. Honestly, we took for granted the bounty around us. As North Carolinians have done for generations, I brake for farmers' markets, where I find fresh, locally-grown produce to turn into tasty, colorful side dishes before the sun sets. The tradition of growing vegetables and fruits close to home is a long one in our state. When Europeans arrived in North Carolina, they found that Native Americans tilled small gardens close to their huts, where they grew pumpkins, sunflowers, corn, squash, beans, gourds, melons, sweet potatoes, and tomatoes.

During the eighteenth century, every home relied on its kitchen garden, since most North Carolinians lived on small farms and had to be self-sufficient. By the nineteenth century, however, large farm cultivation began to develop as the industrial revolution spread. Cities with growing populations emerged to provide labor to factories and businesses. Small farms and gardens declined until the early twentieth century. When food shortages occurred during World War I, so many volunteers actively participated in an effort to reintroduce the vegetable garden in America that the National War Garden Community reported, "The people of this country in 1917 produced a crop valued at $350 million dollars in backyards, vacant lots, and previously uncultivated land."

The same national growing spirit emerged again during World War II, when over 20,000,000 proud Americans grew Victory Gardens; they produced forty percent of the food they consumed and prevented shortages by growing gardens in cities as well as rural areas. Food shortages occurred after the war, however, as Victory Gardens were no longer thought to be necessary and were not planted in 1946.

Until 1950, more North Carolinians were employed on farms than in any other occupation. As times changed, young people began to find jobs in towns and cities. Farmers may have left the country, but you couldn't take the country out of the new suburbanites, who grew rows of fresh tomatoes, beans, strawberries, blueberries, cucumbers, lettuce, parsley, potatoes, and many other foods right in their own backyards. Of course, families brought their heirloom recipes to live in the cities too.

TOMATOES
By Peggy Ann Leu Shriver

Past our sentinel tomatoes
Tramp dusty, bare, brown feet.
Below the hill
"Out of sight—
Out of mind."
Huddle dusty, bare, brown huts.
An odd parade, these neighbors:
Old little girls in tired cottons,
Rummage-sale mothers
Withered and boney,
Broken-arched and heavy,
Dragging tired, dusty, brown feet home.
"You got mighty nice 'maters!"
"I sure could use some 'maters...."
Why do I hesitate
To hand out tomatoes,
To dole out tomatoes
When I've more than enough for my own?

Perhaps it is that I know
  Pride has been broken—
Just for tomatoes.
  Can my hands,
  My white hands
Heal my neighbors' hurt . . . with tomatoes?

Salads are so easy to make that they've been staples on Southern tables for generations. Here are some samples from Leone Epperson's handwritten collection compiled during the 1920s:

<u>*TOMATO SALAD*</u>
Peel and slice five tomatoes nearly to the stem end, press slightly open and insert between the divisions alternate slices of hard boiled eggs and sliced cucumbers. Top with mayonnaise. Sprinkle with chopped olives and serve on lettuce leaf.

Leone's book includes a lovely, handwritten recipe scrawled using a quill pen by her Aunt Minnie. The writing has turned brown with age, but you can clearly read the recipe for cole slaw:

Sliced cabbage	*Pecans*
Chopped apples	*Pineapple*
Chopped celery	*Green peppers*

Mix with cream, sugar, vinegar, or lemon juice, or Salad Dressing.

Immaculate Heart of Mary Church in High Point created a cookbook in 1949 called Kooking Knacks that includes this recipe for macaroni salad contributed by Mrs. A. W. Byerly:

1 box shell macaroni

4 small green onions

1 large green pepper (chopped)

½ teaspoon salt

4 small raw carrots (sliced)

1 small can pimento (chopped)

3 stalks celery cut fine

Cook the macaroni in water salted to taste for 15 minutes. Drain, let cold water run through it, drain and cool. Add other ingredients, serve on chilled lettuce with mayonnaise. Serves 6.

This chapter is full of wholesome recipes made from fresh fruits and vegetables. Also, salads aren't just a pretty pile of leaves any more either. Many in this collection are colorful and sport extravagant textures, from Helen Cochrane's marinated broccoli and cauliflower to Wanda Brooks' hearty German potato salad. There are salads named for the places where they originated, like Asheville salad, a congealed mixture of cream cheese and vegetables, and Polly Barnard's Hoke County turkey salad. There are recipes ranging from bean and macaroni salads to applesauce, and old favorites like egg and shrimp salads. Cranberries are so popular that there are three recipes, one for cranberry salad, another for the time-honored traditional sauce, and my own spicy cranberry version. Chicken salads continue to be perennial favorites. There's conventional chicken salad, popular since the 1800s, and a dressed-up Polynesian version. Colorful, wholesome, and a pleasure to prepare, salads can be side or main dishes. Whether you grow the ingredients yourself, purchase them from local vendors, or shop in modern stores, there are recipes for any occasion. Many are great selections for inexperienced cooks, or people who like to eat at home but are often short on time.

❧ Vegetable Salads ❧

Asparagus Pasta Salad

FOY ALLEN EDELMAN, Lenoir County

Pasta cooked al dente simply means to remove it from boiling water while it's still solid enough to be chewy, not mushy. One way to test pasta for this quality is to remove a small piece and throw it against a firm, vertical surface. If it sticks, it's ready. Adding pasta cooked al dente gives the salad a robust texture. Preparing it a day in advance so that the dressing is absorbed into the pasta also enhances the taste of this salad.

4 ounces fettuccini or thin spaghetti
¼ cup vinegar
3 tablespoons salad oil
1 clove garlic, minced, or 1 teaspoon garlic powder
1 teaspoon oregano
½ teaspoon marjoram
salt and pepper, to taste
12 ounces fresh asparagus, cooked and bias cut
12 cherry tomatoes, quartered
½ cup sliced olives
3 tablespoons parsley, chopped

PREPARE the pasta by cooking according to package directions. Remove when al dente, drain, and rinse with cold water. Chill. For the dressing, combine vinegar, oil, garlic, oregano, marjoram, salt, and pepper. Blend until smooth. Combine the asparagus, tomatoes, olives, and parsley with the pasta. Mix well, then pour the dressing over all.

Serves 4 to 6

Easy Three Bean Salad

FOY ALLEN EDELMAN, Lenoir County

Good picnic or patio dish.

*14 to 16 ounces green beans,
    cooked, drained, and cut into
    bite-sized pieces
14 to 16 ounces yellow beans,
    cooked, drained, and cut into
    bite-sized pieces
14 to 16 ounces kidney beans,
    cooked and drained*

*1 green pepper, sliced in thin
    rings, then in half
1 medium onion, chopped
¼ cup sugar
1 cup apple vinegar
1½ cups vegetable oil
½ teaspoon dry mustard
1 teaspoon salt*

COMBINE beans, green pepper, and onion in large bowl. In a separate bowl, combine the sugar, vinegar, oil, mustard, and salt. Stir until smooth. Pour over the vegetables. Toss gently. Cover and chill well before serving. Stir salad several times while vegetables are marinating.

Serves 6 to 8

Marinated Broccoli and Cauliflower

HELEN COCHRANE, Guilford County

*1 bunch fresh broccoli
1 head cauliflower
1 small onion, chopped
1 cup apple cider vinegar
1 tablespoon sugar*

*1 tablespoon dill
1 tablespoon salt
1 teaspoon black pepper, ground
1 clove garlic, minced
1½ cups salad oil*

CUT BROCCOLI and cauliflower into bite-sized pieces; put into a salad bowl with the onion, and stir until well mixed. Combine remaining ingredients in a separate bowl. Stir until blended, then pour over vegetables in the salad bowl. Stir until all the vegetables are coated. Refrigerate for 24 hours. Drain and serve.

Serves 8 to 10

Marinated Cole Slaw

SARAH SAWYER ALLEN, Lenoir County

1 large cabbage, shredded
1 large onion, chopped
1 large green pepper, chopped
¾ cup vegetable oil
½ cup sugar

1 cup apple cider vinegar
1 teaspoon salt
1 teaspoon dry mustard
½ teaspoon celery seed

MIX THE CABBAGE, onion, and green pepper together well in a large salad bowl. In a 1-quart saucepan combine the vegetable oil, sugar, vinegar, salt, mustard, and celery seed. Bring to a boil, then remove from burner. When cool, pour the oil mixture over the raw vegetables. Refrigerate a day before serving. Slaw will keep for a week in refrigerator.

Serves 8

Blender-made Red Slaw

WANDA BROOKS, Stanly County

1 medium-sized head red cabbage,
  coarsely cut
½ cup sweet pickle relish, or sweet
  pickles, chopped
black pepper, to taste
1 teaspoon salt
½ cup sugar
½ cup vinegar

PUT CABBAGE into your blender. Cover with water, then chop until cabbage is cut into the size pieces you prefer for slaw. Drain and pour into a bowl. Add pickles, seasonings, sugar, and vinegar. Mix until well blended. Refrigerate.

Serves 8 to 10

Aunt Lucille's Oriental Salad

BRENDA ENNIS BYRD, Johnston County

"My Aunt Lucille has taken this salad to as many Johnson family reunions as I can remember," Brenda told me. "So about five years ago, I asked her for the recipe, because I thought it was so delicious. Lucille is a Wake County girl raised up on Sauls Road off of Highway 1010. Her father was Earnest Sauls, a big farmer with lots of land on Sauls Road. I thank my aunt for this food treasure that my family has enjoyed for years." You can substitute packaged slaws for the cabbage and broccoli.

1 cup cabbage, chopped

1 cup broccoli, grated

6 green onions, chopped

2 packages (3 ounces each) Ramen
   Chicken Noodles

3 ounces almonds, slivered

¼ cup sunflower seeds

1 stick (½ cup) margarine

½ cup sugar

1 cup canola oil

¼ cup red vinegar

MIX THE CABBAGE, broccoli, and onions together in a large salad bowl. Separate the flavoring package from the noodles. Combine the noodles (without the flavoring package), almonds, sunflower seeds, and margarine in a frying pan over medium heat. While it browns, make a sauce by stirring the seasoning package contents from the noodles, sugar, oil, and vinegar together. Blend until smooth. When the noodles mixture has browned, remove from heat, and mix with the sauce. When you're ready to serve, pour the noodles mixture over the fresh vegetables in the salad bowl. Serve immediately.

Serves 8

Kraut Salad

MARY DEAL, Rowan County

½ cup salad oil

½ cup apple vinegar

1 cup sugar

1 cup celery

½ cup red sweet pepper, chopped

½ cup green sweet pepper, chopped

1 small onion, chopped

2 cups bean sprouts, drained

4 cups sauerkraut

1 cup water chestnuts, sliced

MAKE A DRESSING for the salad by combining salad oil, vinegar, and sugar in a saucepan. Heat slowly until smooth and blended. Set aside to cool. Combine celery, red and green peppers, onion, bean sprouts, sauerkraut, and water chestnuts in a salad bowl. Pour chilled dressing over salad and refrigerate. Drain liquid before serving.

Serves 8 to 10

Copper Pennies Salad

PHYLLIS LOONEY, Pasquotank County

"This recipe is from Betty Morgan Turner from Elizabeth City," Phyllis told me.

2 pounds fresh carrots	*tomato soup*
1 large onion, peeled and sliced thinly into rings	*¼ cup sugar*
	½ cup vegetable oil
1 large bell pepper, sliced into thin strips	*1 tablespoon dry mustard, optional*
1 can (10.75 ounces) cream of	*¼ cup vinegar*

CLEAN AND PEEL the carrots. Cut into ½-inch rounds; then parboil them until just tender. Remove from heat and drain. Layer the carrots, onions, and bell peppers in a salad bowl. Set aside while you combine the tomato soup, sugar, vegetable oil, mustard, and vinegar in a small saucepan. Heat slightly for thorough mixing. When completely blended, remove from heat, and let cool. Pour over vegetables and refrigerate until serving.

Serves 8

Lemon Onion Salad

MILDRED COTTON, Lee County

1 package (3 ounces) lemon flavored gelatin
1 cup boiling water
1½ cups cottage cheese

1 cup mayonnaise
1 cup celery, finely chopped
½ cup onions, grated
½ cup green pepper, finely chopped

DISSOLVE GELATIN in boiling water. Let it cool slightly. Add remaining ingredients, then stir until well blended. Pour into a mold. Chill until firm.

Serves 6 to 8

Easy Potato Salad

YVONNE JACKSON MULLEN, Pasquotank County

"This is a recipe that my mom, Mattie Taylor Jackson, fixed. Whenever there was a family function or revival at church, they would ask her to make potato salad," Yvonne told me.

½ cup pickle cubes
2 tablespoons prepared mustard
½ cup salad dressing or mayonnaise
1 tablespoon sugar

2 teaspoons celery seed, divided
3 eggs, hard cooked
2 pounds of your favorite white
   potatoes, boiled, peeled, and
   diced

COMBINE the pickle cubes, mustard, salad dressing, sugar, and 1 teaspoon celery seed. Blend until smooth. Dice two of the eggs, then combine with the potatoes in a salad bowl. Pour the pickle mixture over it. Slice the other egg and garnish. Sprinkle with remaining celery seed.

Serves 6 to 8

German Potato Salad

WANDA BROOKS, Stanly County

> *7 or 8 medium white potatoes*
> *1 medium white onion, peeled*
> *and chopped*
> *2 tablespoons, or more if needed,*
> *mayonnaise*
>
> *2 strips bacon, fried and chopped,*
> *reserving the bacon grease*
> *1 to 2 tablespoons cooking oil*
> *1 tablespoon vinegar*

BOIL POTATOES in their skins. When cooked, let them cool, then peel, and slice evenly about 1/8 inch thick. Add onion to potatoes with 2 tablespoons mayonnaise. Mix well. Add the chopped bacon and bacon grease to the salad. Blend in the cooking oil and vinegar. Make sure all the potatoes are covered. Add more mayonnaise if needed. Serve warm.

Serves 8

Macaroni Salad

FOY ALLEN EDELMAN, Lenoir County

I've been trading recipes with other cooks since I was ten years old. Over the years, some were handwritten, some mimeographed, others typed, and now many are sent to me through email on my computer. This is one of the recipes that came to me on an index card handwritten in blue ink, probably using a Bic ballpoint pen, and taped into my recipe scrapbook. The writing looks familiar, meaning I collected it before everyone had a computer at home; unfortunately, however, this cook didn't sign the card. It's still a tasty memory of many shared tables and friendly meals. This is a flexible salad; you can add some chopped ham, chicken, or seafood if you prefer a heavier dinner salad.

1 cup macaroni, cooked and drained
1 cup celery, chopped
½ green pepper, chopped
2 green onion stalks, chopped
¾ cup mayonnaise
½ cup pimentos, diced

½ cup sour cream
2 tablespoons apple vinegar
¼ cup parsley, chopped
½ cup cheddar cheese, diced
salt, pepper, and seasoning salt, to taste

COMBINE all ingredients. Refrigerate any leftovers.

Serves 4

Rice Salad

· ·

HELEN COCHRANE, Guilford County

This recipe was recorded on yellow paper used in kindergarten for children to learn to write on. "Don't use instant rice," Helen warns.

1 cup regular rice
3¾ cups vegetable or chicken broth
6 ounces marinated artichokes
¼ cup green pepper, chopped

½ teaspoon dill weed
½ cup mayonnaise
salt and pepper, to taste
¼ cup olives, sliced, optional

BOIL RICE, covered, in vegetable or chicken broth until soft. Remove from heat. Blend in artichokes, green pepper, dill weed, and mayonnaise. Season to taste. Add olives. Chill and serve.

Serves 6

Easy Marinated Mushrooms

· ·

SALLY CREECH, Johnston County

"Good side dish with beef," says Sally.

2 cans (6 ounces each) button mushrooms or 1½ cups fresh button mushrooms
1/3 cup oil
1 teaspoon salt

2 tablespoons mustard
1 tablespoon brown sugar
1 small onion, thinly sliced

If using fresh mushrooms, wash them well, then place them in a saucepan and bring to a boil. Immediately remove from heat, drain, and cool. Combine all other ingredients. Refrigerate overnight, if possible.

Makes 4 servings

Summer Snap Bean Salad

KATHERINE SAWYER WARD, Bertie County

"Big summer dish!" says Katherine. "They're even better if you can leave them to soak for two nights before serving."

2 pounds fresh snap beans	*1 bottle (16 ounces) Italian*
1 cup of your favorite salad oil	*dressing, Katherine prefers fat*
1 cup cider vinegar	*free style*
¼ cup sugar or fructose	*2 cucumbers*
1 clove garlic	*2 medium onions*

Wash beans well, snap off ends. Parboil in slightly salted water until tender and crisp.

DRAIN in colander, then place in salad bowl. Add oil, vinegar, sweetener, garlic, and Italian dressing. Peel cucumbers before cutting them into thin slices. Add cucumbers to mixture and toss all well. Peel onions, then slice into rings. Separate onion rings, and arrange over green beans. Cover salad bowl, and let stand in refrigerator one night. This allows the vegetables to absorb the flavors but keeps them crisp and fresh. When ready to serve, drain vegetables in a colander.

Serves 8

Easy Spinach Salad

SARAH SAWYER ALLEN, Lenoir County

To clean fresh spinach, separate the leaves. Fill your sink with 2 to 3 inches of cold water sprinkled with salt. Press the leaves into the water one at a time. If the leaves were just picked from a garden, you may need to empty the sink and refill it, sprinkle again with salt, and wash the leaves until you don't feel any grit on the leaves or see any grains of sand on the bottom of the sink.

8 ounces fresh spinach, well cleaned
1 cup bean sprouts
1 cup water chestnuts, drained
1 red onion, sliced
3 hard cooked eggs, peeled and sliced

6 to 8 slices bacon, fried crispy and crumbled
spinach salad dressing (for recipe see the Gravies, Sauces, Marinades, and Salad Dressings chapter)

Combine all ingredients in your favorite salad bowl.

Serves 6 to 8

Tomato Aspic Jelly

LEONE EPPERSON, Durham County

I can't imagine a diet that doesn't include traditional foods. Collecting the foods from local sources, preparing them in long-established seasonal routines, and tasting those flavors that are icons of home all add up to the harmony that characterizes my life. This is one such food that has a distinctive texture, as well as flavor. While I boast of having literally hundreds of North Carolina cookbooks in my personal collection, the earliest recipe I can find by a North Carolinian for tomato aspic is in a 1911 copy of Hibriten Cook Book, compiled by the "Ladies of the Reformed Church" in Lenoir:

Soak one-half box gelatin in one-half cup cold water, dissolve, put in three cups of boiling highly seasoned tomatoes, strain and mold in cups and when chilled and firm serve on lettuce with mayonnaise dressing.

Mrs. K. A. Link

Leone's recipe, recorded in the 1920s, looks almost like ours today. Cooks from then until now have made, enjoyed, shared, and recorded similar combinations of gelatin, tomatoes, and seasoning, making this one of our favorite Southern salads. "Serve on lettuce with mayonnaise," adds Leone in a note.

a little salad oil (or you can use a non-stick cooking spray)
1 envelope (1 ounce) Knox gelatin
½ cup cold water
1 can (14.5 ounces) puréed tomatoes, or equivalent tomato or vegetable juice

1 lemon, juiced
salt and pepper, to taste
½ cup onion, chopped, optional
½ cup celery, chopped, optional
½ cup nuts, chopped, optional
½ cup green olives stuffed with pimentos, sliced, optional

LIGHTLY OIL a mold or other dish with salad oil, or you can use a non-stick cooking spray. Dissolve gelatin in cold water. When the gelatin is soft, blend in the tomatoes and lemon juice; add the seasonings. Pour into prepared dish; refrigerate for 1 hour. Remove from refrigerator, and gently blend in the onion, celery, nuts, and olives. Refrigerate until set.

Serves 4 to 6

Dottie's Harlequin Salad

FOY ALLEN EDELMAN, New Hanover County

I lived in New Hanover County during the 1970s. While everyone knows that coastal cooks are famous for their seafood, perhaps not everyone knows that New Hanover County has many, many fabulous and well-rounded cooks. Dottie Benz and her mother, Betty Crouch, are two such cooks, as is Dottie's brother, Fred, who owns a restaurant in Carolina Beach. This eye-catching and tasty salad is just one of the fancy dishes I have enjoyed with the Crouch family over the years.

1 package (14 to 16 ounces) frozen mixed vegetables
¼ cup onion, grated
¾ cup mayonnaise

lettuce leaves, washed, drained, and chilled
1 cup pickled beets, sliced
parsley to garnish

COOK the vegetables according to package directions, rinse with cold water, and drain well. Stir the onion and mayonnaise into the vegetables until well blended. Line a salad bowl with lettuce leaves. Pour the vegetables over the lettuce. Arrange the beet slices around the top of the vegetables, then garnish with the parsley. Chill and serve.

Serves 8

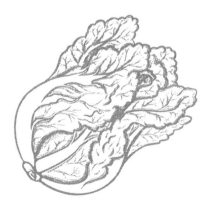

Asheville Salad

SALLY CREECH, Johnston County

non-stick cooking oil

1 can tomato soup, undiluted

2 tablespoons gelatin dissolved in
    ¼ cup water

6 ounces cream cheese, softened to
    room temperature

1 cup mayonnaise, Sally prefers
    Duke's

1½ cups diced celery

¼ cup green pepper, chopped

¼ cup onions, grated

½ cup nuts, chopped

YOU CAN USE a large mold or dish for this salad, or you can use small, individual serving sized molds. Either way, spraying the molds with a little non-stick cooking oil will help them stay perfectly formed when removed from the molds. Heat soup but do not boil. Add dissolved gelatin; stir until smooth. Mix cream cheese and mayonnaise together until completely blended, then combine with soup mixture. Stir in vegetables and nuts until evenly distributed. Pour into prepared container and refrigerate until congealed. Do not freeze. Remove from molds before serving.

Serves 4

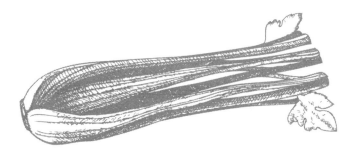

Layered Salad

BRENDA HOWELL, **Wayne County**

Green, crunchy, orange, red, soft, and fresh, fresh, fresh! This multi-colored, many-textured salad is fun to prepare. It fills your kitchen with the fresh garden fragrances that invite guests to the table like a clover blossom attracts bees. I've tried it with an additional layer of field peas and enjoyed the flavor and protein.

1 head lettuce, shredded
1 cup bell pepper, chopped
1 cup celery, chopped
1 cucumber, sliced thin
1 cup carrots, shredded
6 hard cooked eggs, peeled and
*   chopped*

1 ½ cups mayonnaise
1 teaspoon seasoned salt
½ cup bacon bits
½ cup small garden peas
1 cup cherry tomatoes, sliced in
*   half*
1 cup cheddar cheese, grated

USE A LARGE, flat bowl or dish to layer lettuce, bell pepper, celery, cucumber, carrots, and eggs. Combine mayonnaise and salt; then spread over the layers. Arrange the bacon, garden peas, tomatoes, and cheese over the top. Refrigerate overnight, if you can wait.

Serves 12

❧ Fruit Salads ❧

Applesauce

FOY ALLEN EDELMAN, Lenoir County

When my daughter, Harper, was a baby, she absolutely loved fruit. I often enjoyed preparing simple recipes such as combining plain yogurt and bananas in the blender, or this traditional favorite. You can use any apples, like yellow transparent, or green, stamen, or summer rainbow. It's fun to experiment.

5 pounds of your favorite apples *sugar to taste*
water to cover them *sprinkle of cinnamon*

BE SURE to sample some while you peel, core, and quarter the apples. Fill a large kettle; I use a Dutch oven, not quite half full of the apples. Add just enough water to see it; don't cover the apples. Cook over medium heat until tender. If you're using yellow apples, they'll be transparent. Remove from heat, and mash them like you would potatoes. You can use a potato masher, a food mill, or a blender if you like it really smooth. Begin adding sugar to taste, starting with 1 cup. Keep tasting and adding sugar until you get the flavor you prefer. Freeze in plastic containers. Sprinkle with cinnamon when serving.

Makes 2 quarts

Fresh Apple Salad

HILDA G. MCBANE, Chatham County

1 can (20 ounces) crushed pine-
    apple
2/3 cup sugar
1 package (3 ounces) lemon
    gelatin
1 package (8 ounce) cream cheese,
    softened

1 cup of your favorite apples,
    unpeeled, cored, and diced
1 cup celery, chopped
½ cup raisins
½ cup pecans, chopped
1 to 2 cups whipped cream or
    topping

COMBINE pineapple and sugar in a saucepan. Boil for 3 minutes and remove from heat. Add gelatin and stir until dissolved. Blend in the softened cream cheese. Cool thoroughly. Stir in apples, celery, raisins, and nuts. Blend in whipped cream and mix well. Refrigerate and enjoy!

Serves 6 to 8

Easy Waldorf Salad

LEONE EPPERSON, Durham County

This is an especially crisp salad for cold weather meals. It's nice served on lettuce and with ham.

1 cup apples, cored and diced
1 cup celery, chopped
1 cup nuts, chopped

¾ cup mayonnaise or salad
    dressing

COMBINE all ingredients. Chill and serve. Refrigerate leftovers, if you have any!

Serves 6

Grandma's Cranberry Salad

MARIAN MOSS, Granville County

"Cranberry salad was something my husband's mother always made. He never gets tired of it," Marian said. "It's a 'must' at our house for Thanksgiving especially."

2 packages (3 ounces each) straw-
*   berry gelatin*
¾ cup boiling water
½ cup sugar
1 cup orange juice
1 can (14 ounces) whole cranberry
*   sauce*

1 large can (20 ounces) pineapple
*   tidbits, drained*
1 can (11 ounces) mandarin
*   oranges, drained*
2 apples, finely chopped
1 cup nuts, chopped

DISSOLVE gelatin in boiling water. When thoroughly softened, add sugar and orange juice. Blend in cranberry sauce; you can use a potato masher to separate the sauce if you need to. When the cranberry sauce is completely blended with gelatin mixture, add the pineapple, mandarin oranges, apples, and nuts. Stir until well distributed. Chill until gelatin is firm.

Serves 8

Easy Traditional Cranberry Sauce

KATHERINE SAWYER WARD, Bertie County

"This sauce makes great sandwiches with turkey, lettuce, cranberry sauce, and mayonnaise," my cousin Katherine told me.

3 cups fresh, raw cranberries   *sugar or fructose to taste*

POUR CRANBERRIES into a 1-quart saucepan. Cover with water. Boil until berries begin to pop. Add a little more water and remove a tablespoon full to cool. When cool, taste the berries and begin adding sweetener. When berries have absorbed the sweetener, remove another spoonful to taste before adding more. Let cool before serving.

Makes 1½ cups

Spiced Cranberry Sauce

FOY ALLEN EDELMAN, Lenoir County

"This looks very nice when served garnished with a little fresh mint and orange peel."

4 cups raw cranberries
2 cups brown sugar
1 cup orange juice
2 oranges
2 teaspoons ground cloves

1 cup Alize Red Passion Liqueur
or cognac, optional
more sugar, if needed
1 cup toasted, coarsely chopped
walnuts, optional

MIX the cranberries, brown sugar, and orange juice together in 2-quart saucepan. Grate the orange peels, and add the peel to the cranberry mixture. Cut the oranges in half, squeeze out the juice, and add the juice to the cranberries. Heat the saucepan over medium heat until the mixture begins to bubble. Cook around 20 minutes, or until all the cranberries pop. Stir in the liqueur and cloves. Taste to see if the cranberries are so tart that extra sweetening is needed. Add more sugar if needed. Remove and discard any orange seeds, then stir in the walnuts, cool, and serve.

Serves 6 to 8

Theresa's Refreshing Fruit Salad

SUE LANGDALE KORNEGAY, Wake County

"You have to try my sister Theresa's fruit salad," Sue enthusiastically confided. "You can substitute fresh fruit for the fruit cocktail, or use cans of tropical fruit mixture," she continued. "I often double the recipe, because it's so good!" And she was right! This salad is a popular one to take to any covered dish occasion.

1 can (20-ounces) crushed pine-
apple
1/3 cup sugar
1 tablespoon all-purpose flour
1 egg, beaten slightly
2 tablespoons orange juice
1 tablespoon lemon juice

1 teaspoon vegetable oil
1 can (17 ounces) fruit cocktail,
drained
1 can (11 ounces) mandarin
oranges, drained
1 banana, sliced
½ cup heavy creamed, whipped

DRAIN THE PINEAPPLE, reserving 1 cup juice in a saucepan. Make a sauce by combining the pineapple juice with the sugar, flour, egg, orange juice, lemon juice, and the oil. Bring it to a boil, stirring constantly for 1 minute. Remove from heat; cool completely. In a large bowl, combine the crushed pineapple, fruit cocktail, mandarin oranges, and bananas. Fold in the cooled sauce and whipped cream. Refrigerate over night.

Serves 6 to 8

Egg, Chicken, & Turkey Salads

Peppy Pickled Egg Salad

LYNN WILLIAMS, Wayne County

The hard cooked eggs will peel better if you drop them into ice water to chill them immediately after they've cooked. The shells will crack and move away from the solid whites and yolks, making them much easier to separate. "This makes terrific sandwiches with a crisp lettuce leaf," says Lynn.

4 large eggs
½ cup mayonnaise
½ cup celery, finely chopped
¼ cup red onion, minced

¼ cup pickle relish, drained
¼ cup pickled banana peppers, finely chopped
salt and pepper, to taste

PUT THE EGGS in a pot; cover them with cold water, and bring to a rapid boil for 4 minutes. Then turn off the heat, and cover the pot, leaving the pot on the burner. After the eggs sit for 8 minutes, pour the water off and run them under cold water until they have cooled, then peel and chop them. Stir mayonnaise, celery, onion, pickle relish, banana peppers, and eggs together until well blended. Season well. Be sure to refrigerate leftovers, if there are any.

Serves 4

Traditional Chicken Salad

MRS. RUTH CHERRY AND MRS. MARY ELLA JOYNER,
Pleasant Hill Extension Club, Edgecombe County

5 pound hen, or other chicken pieces to make 5 pounds
salt and pepper
2½ cups drained sweet pickles, chopped or sweet pickle relish

½ head celery, chopped fine
6 hard cooked eggs, chopped
2 cups mayonnaise
a little sugar

COOK THE CHICKEN on top of the stove by seasoning it with salt and pepper, then covering it with water. Boil over medium heat until the meat begins to fall off the bone. Remove the pot from the stove, remove the chicken, drain it, and let it cool. Next remove and discard the skin and bones. Chop the meat into small pieces. If this is done with a food processor, be sure to leave solid pieces of chicken, or the salad will be mushy. Place the meat, pickles, celery, eggs, and mayonnaise in a large bowl and mix well. Add salt, pepper, and sugar, to taste. Store in refrigerator. If salad seems too dry, add more mayonnaise.

Makes about 4 pints

Polynesian Chicken Salad

MARY DEAL, Rowan County

"I was born at home on a 100-acre farm in Rowan County [in 1912]. We grew everything we ate on the farm. I had six brothers and two sisters. We all went to college. When one finished, they'd help the next one. Five of us were teachers. I went to Appalachian [now Appalachian State University]," Mary told me. "I taught in Rowan County schools for thirty-six years. My husband, Ralph, and I traveled all over the world. We've been in sixty-eight countries," she continued. "We were in the civil service in Hawaii for two years during World War II. Ralph was a welder. The navy came to him in 1943 up in Baltimore, Maryland—that's where we were then; he worked at Bethlehem Steel's shipyards there—because they wanted him to go to Pearl Harbor. They wanted him to repair ships and asked if he would go. He said he would go if I could go, and they said after he stayed for three months, then I could join him. So he went ahead, and when the three months were up, I went. I went in a convoy of five ships. I was on the ship with the captain of the convoy. We had a destroyer escort for all ten days we were at sea to get to Hawaii. I was afraid. I wore a life jacket, and it had a knife, a whistle, and a flashlight in case we were torpedoed. That would help to protect us, and we had to wear that day and night.

"We worked ten and twelve hours a day when we got there," she continued. "Even if there were warning sirens, you still had to go to work. We had air raids at night. You couldn't get away for a vacation unless you had a health problem. You were stuck there. I worked in the design section where they stored the blueprints for all the ships. I could tell how and where they were damaged by what kinds of prints they wanted when they came into the harbor. And it was my responsibility to lock up the vault at night, and I always said to Ralph, 'If I don't come home at night, come to the vault, and get me, because I was afraid I'd lock myself up in the vault [by accident].'

"We ate in the navy yard part of the time. They had food just like we have here, and they gave you so much I had to turn away, because I didn't want to waste it. And I did part of the cooking. We traded with a Japanese couple who lived close to us. They had a market. Meat was rationed, but they always saved us some. We were lucky; they were very nice to us. You could get all kinds of bananas, coconuts. We had papaya and mango trees in our yard.

"Ralph worked on the USS Missouri when the hull was cracked. He worked three months, twelve hours a day, until it was repaired. And it went back out into service, and that's where the Japanese signed the surrender terms [at the end of the war]. It came back to Pearl Harbor while we were still there, and Ralph was chosen to take up the teak deck to put a plague down to mark the spot where the war in the Pacific ended. The captain and Ralph each had a piece of the teakwood to take home. We had it for many years, but Ralph wanted to take it back to Hawaii; so we took it back to the museum on the Missouri there.

"This is one of the recipes I collected while we lived there."

3 cups cooked chicken, diced *½ cup sour cream*
2 cups celery, diced *1 teaspoon lemon juice*
1 cup white grapes, cut in half *1 teaspoon salt*
1 cup pineapple tidbits, drained *1½ teaspoons curry*
½ cup carrots, grated *½ cup sliced almonds*
1 cup mayonnaise

COMBINE chicken with celery, grapes, pineapple, and carrots. In a separate bowl, blend mayonnaise and sour cream together with the lemon juice, salt, and curry until smooth, then pour over the chicken mixture. Just before serving, sprinkle with the almonds.

Serves 6 to 8

Hoke County Turkey Salad

POLLY BARNARD, Hoke County

"Since House of Raeford, a turkey producer, was located in Hoke County for so long, I'm giving you a turkey salad recipe," Polly told me. "This is very good served as a luncheon dish with crackers. It makes a complete meal by adding a dessert."

*2½ cups cooked, cooled white
   meat (turkey or chicken may be
   used)
½ cup tidbit pineapple, drained
½ cup English walnuts, coarsely
   broken
½ cup white raisins*

*1½ ribs of celery, coarsely chopped
4 tablespoons mayonnaise
½ teaspoon salt
dash paprika
grapes for garnish
lettuce leaves, for serving*

CUT MEAT in cubes. Combine drained pineapple, walnuts, raisins, and celery in large bowl with meat. Add mayonnaise and toss lightly. Serve on lettuce leaf. Garnish with a dash of paprika, and place white grapes around and over top.

Serves 6

Smoked Turkey and Apricot Salad

LYNN WILLIAMS, Wayne County

2 cups smoked turkey, chopped

1 cup celery, chopped

½ cup dried apricots, chopped

¼ cup sweet pickles, chopped, or
   sweet pickle relish, Lynn prefers
   Mount Olive brand

½ cup radishes, thinly sliced

2 scallions, chopped

½ cup mayonnaise

1 teaspoon celery seed

salt and freshly ground black
   pepper, to taste

romaine lettuce

COMBINE turkey, celery, apricots, pickles, radishes, and scallions in a large bowl. Blend well, and set aside. Whisk mayonnaise, celery seed, salt, and pepper together in a small bowl. Fold dressing into the turkey mixture; toss gently to coat. Taste and correct seasonings. Cover and refrigerate to chill. Serve on romaine lettuce.

Serves 4

❧ Seafood Salads ❧

Crabmeat Mold

. . . .

SARAH SAWYER ALLEN, Lenoir County

Nice served on a bed of lettuce and garnished with olives and parsley.

a little salad oil or non-stick cook-
ing spray
3 ounces unflavored gelatin, Sarah
prefers Knox
1 cup cold water
12 ounces cream cheese, softened to
room temperature
½ cup cream of celery soup
1 cup mayonnaise
1 small onion, chopped
1 tablespoon Worcestershire sauce
½ teaspoon salt
2 cups crabmeat
1 cup celery, chopped

PREPARE a 2-quart mold by rubbing a little salad oil into it or spraying it with non-stick vegetable oil. Set aside. Stir the gelatin into the cold water. When gelatin has softened, pour it into the top of double boiler. Turn heat to medium. Add the cream cheese, soup, mayonnaise, onion, Worcestershire sauce, and salt. Heat until the whole mixture is blended well. Fold in the crabmeat and celery; stir slowly until well distributed. Remove from heat; pour into prepared mold. Chill until set, about 3 to 4 hours.

Serves 8

Hallie's Easy Shrimp Salad

SALLY CREECH, Johnston County

1 pound shrimp, boiled, peeled,
   and deveined
1 cup celery, chopped
¼ cup stuffed olives, sliced
½ teaspoon onion, minced

½ cup mayonnaise
¼ cup French dressing
Salt, to taste
lemon juice, to taste

Combine all ingredients. Refrigerate leftovers.

Serves 4

New Bern Shrimp Salad

MARY WARD (Foy Allen Edelman's great aunt), Craven County

I am so fortunate to have relatives who value dusty, torn treasures like
a copy of a New Bern cookbook, From the Baron's Kitchen. Written in
the 1950s, it contains many family recipes, including some by my great
aunt, Mary Pickett Ward. We called her Auntie, and she was an amazing
woman. Auntie was born in Kenansville in 1891. Her family moved to
New Bern early in the twentieth century and purchased 509 Pollock Street,
a handsome, late Victorian home built in 1882. Unlike many women of
the time, Auntie graduated from Peace College in Raleigh before earning
a master's degree from the University of North Carolina. She traveled
widely and was in China in 1915 after World War I broke out. Though
Auntie was small in stature, she was a dynamo as far as being a hostess.

She was best known as the hostess for our extended family's Christmas Eve dinner. All the men came dressed in dark, wool suits, and all the ladies arrived in their holiday finery to enjoy dining at her large table set with family silver, linen, and porcelain. Like many, many members of my family, Mary loved and revered history and was one of the first docents at Tryon Place, where staff members today remember her walking down the street in her period dress to perform tours for avid tourists. Here's one of her simple, traditional recipes.

2 pounds of raw shrimp	*6 stalks of crisp celery, chopped*
salt and pepper, to taste	*½ cup sweet pickles, chopped*
¼ cup vinegar	*1 tablespoon prepared mustard*
¼ cup Worcestershire sauce	*½ cup green peppers, chopped*
1½ quarts boiling	*1 cup mayonnaise*

PUT THE SHRIMP, salt, pepper, vinegar, and Worcestershire sauce into the boiling water. Boil for 2 to 3 minutes, until the shrimp turn pink. Remove from heat, pour off the boiling water, and cover the shrimp with cold water. When shrimp are cold enough to handle, peel and devein them. Combine cleaned shrimp with celery, pickles, mustard, green peppers, and mayonnaise. Chill.

Makes 4 servings

Salmon Salad

LEONE EPPERSON, Durham County

Salmon is a flexible ingredient when it comes to flavors. You can try different types of pickles and olives to vary the taste.

1½ cups salmon, skinned and
    filleted
½ cup celery, chopped
lemon juice, to taste
2 hard cooked eggs, chopped

¼ cup pickles, chopped
½ cup olives, chopped
¾ cup salad dressing or mayon-
    naise

DRAIN the salmon. Stir in the celery, lemon juice, eggs, pickles, and olives. When well mixed, add the salad dressing or mayonnaise. Stir until completely blended.

Makes about 2 cups

Easy Traditional Tuna Salad

WANDA BROOKS, Stanly County

"I used to make this when my Daddy and I lived in Cary," Wanda says in a note to her four daughters in her homemade cookbook of family recipes. "Guess it was good for a tight budget," she concluded, and good for you, too.

1 can (7 ounces) tuna
2 eggs, hard cooked and chopped
½ cup celery, chopped
½ teaspoon prepared mustard

¼ cup sweet pickle relish or sweet
    pickles, chopped
½ cup salad dressing or mayon-
    naise

PLACE TUNA in a mixing bowl. Use a fork to break up the chunks, then add eggs, celery, pickles, salad dressing, and mustard. Blend well. Refrigerate any leftovers.

Serves 2

Easy Savory Tuna Fish Salad

FOY ALLEN EDELMAN, Lenoir County

When I was in college at UNC-Wilmington, one of my good friends, Freddie Lyerly, showed me how to make this zesty version of tuna salad.

1 can (5 ounces) tuna fish,
drained
½ cup celery, chopped
1 tablespoon onion, grated

1 tablespoon mustard
½ cup dill pickles, chopped
½ cup mayonnaise

COMBINE all ingredients. Chill and serve. Refrigerate leftovers.

Serves 2

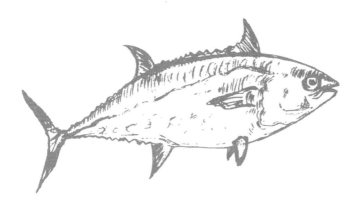

Gravies, Sauces, Marinades, & Salad Dressings

Whats better for adding a distinctive taste to a meal than a homemade gravy, sauce, marinade, or salad dressing? Or, if you're in a hurry, making a sauce at home gives something store-bought an enticing personal touch. To me, a meal simply has not reached its potential without something tangy to spice it up. Sometimes it's savory gravy that wakes up all the goodness in roasted turkey. Other times, it's a sauce, like hollandaise, that adds just the right flavor to steamed vegetables. Perhaps a marinade is just what's needed to make the taste of meat and seafood burst into flavor. A zesty salad dressing infused with herbs is a good complement to an already great bowl of greens. And, quite honestly, if you want to impress your friends with your culinary skills, make one of the "simply" scrumptious recipes in this chapter.

It's ironic that the word "gravy" implies more than just a concoction of flavors that's poured over something, when they're deceptively easy to make, as demonstrated in this recipe from 1948:

Mrs. James G. Dancy, Kannapolis, Cabarrus County, from *The Daily Independent Cook Book 1948: A Collection of Favorite Recipes Tested and Proved in Kannapolis Area Kitchens by Some of North Carolina's Best Cooks.*

1 cup thick gravy made by adding 1 tablespoon flour to broth that chicken was cooked in. Half milk and half broth may be used. Salt to taste.

Gravy, though among the simpler sauces, can take an average meal and send its texture and flavor over the top. This chapter begins with a basic gravy recipe and continues with a variety of gravies useful for poultry, beef, and pork.

In an agricultural state as plentiful as ours, it's easy to take for granted the availability of reasonably priced and good quality chicken, beef, pork, and seafood. Like all good quality foods, these can be easily prepared.

Some ways to keep them from becoming monotonous entrées are to add a sauce or infuse them with a flavorful marinade. North Carolina's culinary heritage is rich with varieties of regional barbecue, and just as abundant are the barbecue sauce recipes. This chapter includes variations popular in mountain, piedmont, and inner coastal plain counties. Savory sauces to accompany vegetables follow. Marinades give meats and seafood new and appealing tastes. You'll find recipes for beef, game, turkey, and shrimp included.

Salad dressings are as diverse as the folks who spread them over their leaves. One very positive quality of preparing foods at home means you know what you're getting. Store-bought salad dressings often contain significant amounts of corn syrup, sugar, and preservatives. Making salad dressings at home is as refreshing as cutting up raw vegetables to make a tossed salad, a feast for the eyes and the nose, as well as the palate. And you can make most salad dressings in a few minutes. Here's a sample that will soon be 100 years old:

COUNTRY CLUB DRESSING
Leone Epperson
Durham County

A small newspaper clipping is pasted on a page in the homemade cookbook Leone Epperson created during the 1920s. "If you have wanted to know how to make the good salad dressing that is served at the Hope Valley Country Club, here is how it's done." Patents for manual, rotary-style eggbeaters are recorded as early as 1865, and what a wonderful invention they were. The Dover eggbeater was advertised in a Sears catalog in 1897 for $.09.

1 cup Wesson oil

½ cup catsup

1-3 cups vinegar

1 tablespoon sugar

1 teaspoon prepared mustard

1-2 teaspoons Worcestershire sauce

1 teaspoon salt

½ teaspoon celery seed

1 tablespoon whole mustard seeds

Beat with Dover eggbeater. Store
    in ice box, shaking each time
    before serving."

Beat with Dover eggbeater. Store in ice box, shaking each time before
serving."

The salad dressing recipes begin with an oil and vinegar base and
branch out into heavier varieties like thousand island and blue cheese.

As icings are to cakes, so the flavorful gravies, sauces, marinades, and
salad dressings in this chapter richly complete many tempting main dishes, vegetables, or salad dishes found in the previous chapters.

❧ Gravy ❧

Basic gravy

One of my vintage cookbooks is Federation of Home Demonstration Clubs Favorite Recipes. The chapter entitled "Sauces" begins with a quote, "A Little Dab Makes All the Difference!" That little dab can be a gravy that enhances and teases out rich flavors just perfectly as finishing touches for meats, potatoes, and rice. Gravy is a simple combination of a fat with starch and liquid, usually a broth, and sometimes spices. It's quick to make, as little as ten to fifteen minutes, and adds robust tastes to already good foods.

Some things to consider while creating your own individual gravy are the types of fats and liquids you might use, drippings you may want to reserve, and the texture you want your gravy to have. For example, you can use butter, lard, fatty pan drippings, or margarine to make gravy, or none at all. If you're going to use lard, I suggest you get it from a source that renders it from pigs raised on pasture and contains no additives. When I was growing up, my mother and our housekeeper saved bacon grease, using bacon from hogs raised locally. They never cooked with packaged lard. If you've never tasted chicken cooked in home-rendered lard or bacon drippings, you might want to go out of your way to find some and prepare the food yourself. The taste is entirely succulent and what many of us remember from our childhoods. I've also known North Carolina cooks who brown flour in a skillet with no fat. Mildred Cotton's turkey gravy is one of these recipes and is found later in this chapter. Regarding the broth, if you've recently cooked a chicken, turkey, beef, or pork roast, you may have some broth available that's perfect for making gravy. When any of these broths get completely cold in the refrigerator, you can lift off the fat from the top. The resulting broth will give you a lighter and clearer gravy. You can purchase canned broth or use the water in which vegetables have been boiled. You can combine liquids such as broth and milk or cream. When I grew up, my mother's signature gravy, made from broth and milk, was thick and white. When I visited Iredell County, I learned that this gravy variation is sometimes referred to as "sawmill gravy" and that if you use water to thicken gravy, it's called "poor man's gravy."

A tip for making oh-so-good, rich, flavorful gravy is to be sure to save the tasty drippings in the bottom of the pan where the meat you've prepared was roasted or fried. Those drippings are full of intense flavor and contain delicious essences from any herbs you added. You can either scrape the drippings from the bottom of the pan into the saucepan where you're preparing your gravy, or pour a little of the gravy into the pan, spreading it over the bottom and sides, then returning it back to the gravy pot.

Gravies can be heavy or light, gray to brown, almost clear or opaque, depending on your preference. The more broth you add to the fat and flour mixture, the lighter the gravy will be. I prefer a smooth, light gravy that's easily absorbed by rice and potatoes. The longer you cook the fat and flour mixture, the darker and thicker the gravy will become. If you've never tried to make gravy before, you can experiment until you get the combination that's just right for your favorite dish.

¼ cup butter, lard, fatty pan
drippings, or margarine
¼ cup all-purpose flour

2-3 cups liquid – you can use
broth, milk, wine, cream, or a
combination

SLOWLY MELT the butter in a saucepan over low heat. When the butter is melted, stir in the flour. Continue stirring while you gradually turn up the heat to medium. As the mixture heats, it will begin to thicken; keep stirring. When it becomes harder to stir, gradually pour in the liquid. Keep stirring. When all the liquid has been absorbed into the butter/flour mixture and the consistency is smooth, remove from heat and serve.

Makes 2 to 3 cups

Turkey Gravy

MILDRED COTTON, Lee County

TAKE THE BROTH out of the turkey or chicken. Let it cool, then remove any fat from the top. Brown the flour in a saucepan. You don't have to use any shortening in it. Use any kind of pan, a black skillet is fine. You just have to let the flour brown. You have to keep stirring it, or it'll burn. "I use low heat, not a real hot heat," Mildred told me. "Let it brown slowly until you get it to the color you'd like the gravy to be. I like mine a good chocolate color. Then you add your broth. If the broth is already seasoned, you don't even have to add salt or pepper. I don't use giblets in mine. I like it just plain. I use sage, salt, and pepper when I cook my turkey. Sometimes I put a little butter inside the turkey. That way, when the essences come off the turkey, the broth has a good flavor for the gravy. I don't make my gravy very thick. I like it where it will spread smoothly over the meat and potatoes and dressing. You can always add more broth if you want it lighter."

Note: if you use quantities suggested in the basic gravy above, you'll make 2 to 3 cups.

Mr. Cannon's Chicken Gravy

BRENDA CANNON BOWERS, Burke County

reserved drippings from chicken	*1 cup milk*
4 to 6 tablespoons all-purpose flour	*1 cup water*

USE DRIPPINGS from frying the chicken for gravy by pouring off most of the oil and leaving the browned flour in the bottom. Add 2 to 3 tablespoons of flour and reheat in the skillet over low to medium heat until the drippings begin to bubble. Continue cooking until the mixture thickens and browns into a thick paste. Combine milk and water before gradually pouring into paste in skillet. Stir slowly and constantly until gravy is smooth. For a lighter gravy, use more milk and water.

Makes 2 cups

Giblet Gravy

LOUISE CROSS (*from The Favorite Recipes of Beck's United Church of Christ*), Davidson County

Drippings are the remains in the bottom of the pan after a chicken or turkey has been roasted or baked, and drippings are where the flavor is concentrated. Louise cooks her giblets separately in water and uses the broth to make her gravy.

5 tablespoons all-purpose flour	*1¾ cups giblet broth (add water,*
salt, to taste	*if needed)*
1¼ cups drippings (add butter or	*giblets, cut up after boiling*
margarine, if needed)	

COMBINE FLOUR and salt in saucepan. Add drippings and slowly heat pan over low heat. Stir until smooth. Keep stirring as you add broth. Slightly increase the heat and continue to stir until thickened. Add giblets.

Makes 2 2/3 cups

Sausage Gravy

FOY ALLEN EDELMAN, **Lenoir County**

This is a great favorite served over hot, split biscuits. You can also make scrumptious, Southern-style eggs benedict by toasting and buttering English muffins and hard cooking eggs. When you're ready to serve, split the muffins. Shell the eggs, and slice them onto the muffins. Pour the gravy over all.

1 pound bulk pork sausage
½ stick (¼ cup) butter or bacon
    drippings
¼ cup all-purpose flour

2 cups milk
red hot pepper sauce, to taste, I
    prefer Texas Pete

BREAK UP THE SAUSAGE and fry it out in a skillet. Remove the sausage and drain it, leaving the essences in the pan. Melt the butter or drippings over low heat until soft. Remove the pan just long enough to stir in the flour, then return to burner. Slowly thicken the mixture until the flour is evenly distributed and smooth. Gradually add the milk, turning up the burner slightly. When all the milk is added and the mixture is smooth, stir in the sausage and Texas Pete.

Serves 4

Red Eye Gravy

JERRY SOUTHARD, Randolph County

"I went to work at Hop's [Bar-b-q] when I was fourteen," Jerry told me. "I learned to cook bar-b-q as a teenager and continued to work at Hop's until I later bought it." It's a favorite, very popular local place in the heart of downtown Asheboro. "It looks just like it did when I first went to work here," Jerry continued. "The interior is the same as it was when I was a teenager."

2 slices of country ham	*½ - ¾ cup premade black coffee,*
a little water, about ½ cup	*percolated or dripped*

Sear the ham in a frying pan; remove it, but leave the grease and ham essence in the pan. Heat the grease. Add the water and stir. When the water has blended with the grease, add some coffee, pour over hot grits.

Serves 2

Tomato Gravy

THE QUAKER COOKBOOK, 1954, Guilford County

A note at the bottom of this recipe tells us that it comes from Westown School. Glennie Beasley, of Chatham County, told me she grew up on a farm in nearby Chatham County. "We dipped our biscuits into tomato gravy," she told me. Though it is not widely used in the United States currently, Spry is a vegetable shortening that was popular during the 1940s. You can substitute another shortening like Crisco for the Spry.

TAKE A LARGE FRYING pan and use a suitable brand of grease (such as Spry). Slice the tomatoes, dredge in flour, and fry. After they are fried, remove about three-fourths of the tomatoes, leaving a few that have, perhaps, started to disintegrate or fall apart. Remove pan from fire, mash tomatoes, stir in a flour [all-purpose] paste, and add pinch of soda. After these are well mixed, milk in the desired quantity is added and the frying pan returned to heat. Caution must be taken that the milk is not boiled and is just brought slowly to a simmer. Add the remaining tomatoes to reheat them. Salt and pepper can be added to season.

⋇ Sauces ⋇

Traditional Eastern North Carolina Barbecue Sauce

MORELAND GUETH, Guilford County

"I learned this recipe from an old college roommate," Moreland told me, "and have played with it over the years. An old boss also used a similar sauce; so it has just kind of evolved. It's a traditional eastern North Carolina barbecue sauce for pigs and chickens. It's simple to make." Born in High Point, Moreland was an employee of the North Carolina Forestry Service. His interests included ax throwing, firefighting, and baking. When bottled, this makes a memorable and appreciated Christmas gift.

1 gallon apple cider vinegar
1 pound brown sugar, optional
1 jar (1.5 ounces) crushed red
   peppers

salt and pepper, to taste
ground cayenne, to taste

Combine all ingredients in a soup pot. Bring to a boil, then let it simmer for at least an hour, stirring occasionally. Sauce is ready to use when crushed red peppers sink to the bottom of the pot. It may be used immediately thereafter, or stored indefinitely in a refrigerator for later use. But watch out – when stored, the sauce gets stronger and that means hotter!

Makes 1 gallon

Thick Barbecue Sauce

MARGUERITE HUGHEY, **Buncombe County**

A typewritten note indicates that Carolyn Anderson gave Marguerite this recipe on Labor Day, 1958. This is a versatile barbecue sauce with the iconic Southern flavor that many Carolinians associate with home and good times. It's great poured over chicken or ribs as they cook. It's also an essential condiment at the table. You can double the recipe and store any leftovers in the refrigerator.

1½ teaspoons salt	*1 small onion, finely chopped*
2 teaspoons pepper	*1 1/3 cups water*
1½ teaspoons paprika	*½ cup vinegar*
sugar, to taste	*Worcestershire sauce, to taste*
½ teaspoon garlic salt	*1 stick (½ cup) butter or marga-*
2/3 cup catsup	*rine*
2/3 cup tomato juice	

COMBINE all ingredients in saucepan. Stir constantly as it simmers over low to medium heat until onions are soft.

Makes about 10 servings

Ray's Barbecue Sauce

ZEB SPEECE, Iredell County

"I worked for the highway department for forty-one years," Zeb told me. "We didn't have any recreation or benefits. We had a monthly salary. I met a man named Ray Stutts back around 1947 or 1948 when he came to work for the department too. He had a homemade grill and a good recipe for barbecue sauce. He said, 'Let's all get together and have a barbecue for Christmas.' So the department bought a bunch of [pork] shoulders. To get the mustard to blend with the other ingredients, you need to mix it with the vinegar, and shake it up until they combine smoothly. If you try to mix it with the catsup without doing that, you'll wear a spoon out."

½ cup apple cider vinegar
½ cup prepared mustard
1 cup Worcestershire sauce
1 cup tomato catsup

1½ cups brown sugar
½ ounce of red hot pepper sauce,
or more if you want it hotter,
Zeb prefers Texas Pete

COMBINE the vinegar and mustard in jar or mixing bowl. Shake or mix with electric mixer until fully combined. Pour into a large saucepan. Add Worcestershire sauce, catsup, brown sugar, and Texas Pete. Bring the entire mixture to a boil. Simmer for at least one hour.

Makes about 1 quart

Tomato Sauce

MARTHA BLAINE WOODS, Macon County

Martha Woods and her husband live in a mountain cabin near the Georgia border. We visited on their front porch where they have a swing big enough for two, where she told me how to make her homemade cabbage soup from this delicious base. "This wonderful, rich tomato blend can be used for a variety of recipes including soup, chili, and tomato sauce," Martha says.

10 to 12 Roma tomatoes

1 to 2 bell peppers, finely chopped

1 medium onion, finely chopped

1 to 2 jalapeño peppers, finely chopped

GRIND fresh Roma tomatoes in blender. Combine tomatoes with peppers, onion, and jalapeños together in large pot on stove. Bring mixture to a frothy boil. Remove from stove, cool, and can according to directions included with the jars.

Makes about a quart

Hollandaise Sauce

FRANKLIN COUNTY

This recipe comes from a cookbook entitled, *Federation of Home Demonstration Clubs Favorite Recipes*. No date is given; no specific cook is named. An advertisement in the first page reads, "VISIT THE FRIENDLY FIRST NATIONAL BANK HENDERSON, N.C. ALL DEPOSITS UP TO $5,000 INSURED BY THE FEDERAL DEPOSIT INSURANCE CORPORATION." This sauce is often used for broccoli, asparagus, and other vegetables.

2 egg yolks, beaten　　　　　*1 tablespoon lemon juice*
¼ teaspoon salt　　　　　　*½ cup boiling water*
1 stick (½ cup) melted butter　*cayenne pepper, to taste*

COMBINE egg yolks with salt, butter, and lemon juice in the top of a double boiler. Stir well, adding the boiling water gradually. Cook until thick and smooth. Add cayenne to taste.

Makes 6 servings

"Hot Dog" Sauce

MRS. R. P. YORK, Cabarrus County

Everybody called this "hot dog chili" when I was growing up. I found this version in The Daily Independent Cook Book 1948: A Collection of Favorite Recipes Tested and Proved in Kannapolis Area Kitchens by Some of North Carolina's Best Cooks.

½ pound ground beef

½ cup tomato catsup

½ ounce chili powder

1 teaspoon sugar

½ cup vinegar

½ cup vegetable oil

2 tablespoons French-style mustard

½ teaspoon cayenne pepper

½ teaspoon black pepper

BROWN the beef in a 2-quart saucepan. Drain off the grease. Add all additional ingredients to the beef. Cook slowly for 1 hour, stirring often.

Enough for 6 to 8 hot dogs

Red Devil Sauce

SARAH SAWYER ALLEN, Lenoir County

This is good served with clams, fritters, and lobster.

1 cup cheddar cheese, grated

1 can (10.75 ounces) cream of
   tomato soup

1 egg, beaten

salt, to taste

cayenne pepper, to taste

COMBINE cheese, soup, and egg in a 1-quart saucepan. Heat on low until mixture thickens. Season. Refrigerate any leftovers.

Makes 6 to 8 servings

Easy Cheese Sauce

FOY ALLEN EDELMAN, Lenoir County

If you use margarine for this sauce, it needs to be a firm one that comes in quarters, not a soft-spread brand. You can use your favorite cheese or a combination of cheeses. The secret is to be patient while you make the roux, the paste made from butter and flour. Make sure the butter is thoroughly melted over low heat. I use one of the new high temperature spatulas to stir so that I can press the flour down into the butter while the sauce thickens. This prevents lumps. However, if you do get lumps, you can always use an electric mixer to smooth them out. After all, lumps don't affect the rich flavor.

½ stick (¼ cup) butter or margarine
¼ cup all-purpose flour
2 cups milk
¾ cup cheese, grated
1 teaspoon dried mustard

red hot pepper sauce, to taste, I
prefer Texas Pete brand
salt and pepper, to taste
a sprinkle of ground nutmeg,
optional

MELT THE BUTTER in a saucepan over low heat. When it is completely melted, remove the pot from the burner just long enough to stir in the flour. Return the pot to the burner and stir until the flour is completely absorbed by the butter and the mixture thickens with no lumps. Keep stirring while you slowly add the milk. When the sauce has absorbed all the milk, keep stirring while you sprinkle in the cheese. When the sauce has absorbed the cheese and is smooth, add the mustard, red hot pepper sauce, salt, pepper, and nutmeg. You can stop stirring now; remove your tasty sauce from the heat and serve. Refrigerate any leftovers.

Makes 3 cups

Cocktail Sauce

North Carolinians across the state love seafood, and what's better to bring out all the subtle flavors in the fish, shrimp, oysters, clams, and crab than a homemade sauce? Cocktail sauces are found in the section of strong reds on North Carolina's culinary palette, but there are many variations, all using a small set of ingredients, but with slightly different colors, textures, strengths, and tastes. Clams, for example, have a stronger taste; a sauce with lots of horseradish and red hot pepper sauce is good with them. That same sauce would overpower the delicate flavor of crab. It's easy to adapt your recipe to work for both. Making the perfect cocktail sauce is more of an adventure than an exact science. Many of my friends and acquaintances have told me that their families make their own sauces, but they don't really have specific recipes. Every person in my nuclear family made a different sauce, but we mostly use the same ingredients. My brothers, Will and Reynold Allen, have always held contests to see who can make the hottest sauce (honestly, they would sweat so much that I'm sure I saw steam coming out of their ears), and the resulting concoctions are excellent. But in the end, each of us prefers our own, so instead of providing you with just one recipe, I'm sharing several. This way, you can either choose one, or scrutinize the ingredients in each of them until you come up with your own combination.

ARAMINTA BLOWE (MY AUNT), Halifax County

½ cup catsup	*1 tablespoon Worcestershire sauce*
2 tablespoons lemon juice	*red hot pepper sauce, to taste*
½ teaspoon salt	*1 teaspoon horseradish sauce*

COMBINE all ingredients. Blend until smooth.

Makes 4 servings

. . . .

TREVA GREER (*from The Favorite Recipes of Beck's United Church of Christ*), Davidson County

Unfortunately, Treva is not one of my relatives. I haven't met her yet, but I have a copy of a cookbook she helped type in Lexington. The book is full of delicious sauces and dips.

½ cup lemon juice	*½ tablespoon horseradish*
½ cup tomato juice	*½ teaspoon salt*
1 tablespoon Worcestershire sauce	

BEAT ALL ingredients together.

Makes 1 cup

Jacki and I have known each other since second grade, so I think that means we're somehow related. "My husband, Tom, shares his recipe with everyone," Jacki told me.

catsup

lemon juice

*horseradish, Tom often uses Ingle-
hoffer brand, but he says there
are other "purer" brands of
horseradish you can use*

*what-dis-here-sauce (Worcester-
shire sauce)*

"Nothing is measured," says Tom. "[It's] all done by taste or sight; all portions are generous."

. . . .

"Just be aware that they don't brand it as ATOMIC Horseradish for nothing," my older brother, Will, told me. "That stuff will take your head off! I love it!" He calls this recipe Spicy Red Cocktail Sauce.

*Very generous quantities of Atomic
brand horseradish sauce (sold
at Fresh Market) - Will uses
the entire bottle to make a big
batch*

*enough catsup to make it a bit
more red than white
juice of one fresh lemon
generous dollops of red hot pepper
sauces, Texas Pete and Tabasco
sauce*

MIX TOGETHER very thoroughly and taste constantly to get the level of spiciness preferred.

Mrs. Watkins' Tartar Sauce

ELIZABETH JONES WATKINS, Bertie County

Lib Watkins was a very special person to me. She was my godmother. Lib made my wedding dress and embroidered it with her own designs. She was artistic in many ways, including painting and cooking. This is just one of her recipes that I still enjoy today.

1 cup mayonnaise, chilled
½ teaspoon onion, minced
½ teaspoon parsley, minced
1 tablespoon sweet cucumber
  pickles, chopped

1 tablespoon capers, chopped
1 tablespoon stoned green olives,
  chopped
1 teaspoon vinegar

BLEND all ingredients together. Chill.

Makes 1½ cups

Remoulade Sauce for Seafood

KITTY BLACK (*from Something Old - Something New from the Women's Club of Clinton, 1975*), Sampson County

You can use dried herbs if you can't get fresh ones.

1 cup mayonnaise
1 tablespoon dill pickle, finely
  chopped
1 tablespoon capers, chopped

1 tablespoon prepared mustard
1 tablespoon parsley, chopped
1 tablespoon tarragon, chopped
1 tablespoon chervil, chopped

COMBINE all ingredients in a food processor. Grind until well blended. Refrigerate.

Makes 1½ cups

❧ Marinades ❧

Tom's Beef Marinade

HELEN COCHRANE, Guilford County

1 small onion, coarsely chopped
1 clove garlic, minced, or 1 teaspoon garlic powder
1/3 cup dry white wine, dry sherry, or wine vinegar
3 tablespoons soy sauce
1 tablespoon honey
1 tablespoon vegetable oil
¼ teaspoon ginger
¼ teaspoon pepper

COMBINE all ingredients in a large bowl. When blended, press beef into the marinade. Refrigerate for 12 to 24 hours. Drain, broil, and slice.

Makes enough to marinate 2 pounds of beef

Easy Marinade for Beef or Game

RICK HAMILTON, Wake County

2 cups dry red wine
2 tablespoons vegetable oil
1 teaspoon black pepper, coarsely ground
2 teaspoons salt
2 medium onions, thinly sliced
1 garlic clove, crushed

COMBINE all ingredients. Add meat, and refrigerate overnight.

Makes enough for 5 pounds of meat

Shrimp Marinade

FOY ALLEN EDELMAN, **Lenoir County**

Use just enough to cover cooked shrimp.

2 cups of your favorite chutney
2 cups vegetable oil
1 cup apple cider vinegar
salt, pepper, red hot pepper, and
Worcestershire sauces, dash of
each
½ cup parsley, coarsely chopped
garlic, to taste

COMBINE all ingredients. Refrigerate.

Makes 5 cups

✌ Salad Dressings ✌

Marie's Light French Dressing

MARGUERITE HUGHEY, **Buncombe County**

You can substitute 4 tablespoons tarragon or garlic-flavored vinegar for the vinegar/tarragon combination below if you prefer a tangier flavor.

1 teaspoon salt
1 teaspoon dry mustard
1 teaspoon celery seed
1 teaspoon paprika
1 teaspoon onion, grated
3 cloves garlic, crushed or finely minced

1 cup olive oil, or your favorite vegetable oil
4 tablespoons mild vinegar and 1 tablespoon tarragon vinegar
sugar, to taste, optional
½ lemon, juiced with seeds removed, optional

MIX salt, mustard, celery seed, paprika, onion, and garlic in mixing bowl. Alternately pour in oil and vinegar blending thoroughly until you get a smooth mixture. Taste, and add sugar accordingly, if desired. Add lemon juice for a lighter, thinner dressing. Keeps well refrigerated in a tightly covered jar.

Makes 1½ cups

Spinach Salad Dressing

SARAH SAWYER ALLEN, Lenoir County

1 cup salad oil
1 cup catsup
1 teaspoon salt
¼ cup apple cider or wine vinegar
3 scallions, finely chopped

1 teaspoon Worcestershire sauce
2 tablespoons sherry
1/3 cup sugar
½ teaspoon paprika

COMBINE all ingredients. Stir until blended.

Serves 8

Easy Thousand Island Salad Dressing

MRS. EDWARD BISSETTE *(Something Old - Something New from the Women's Club of Clinton, 1975)*, Sampson County

1 cup mayonnaise
½ cup catsup or chili sauce
¼ cup sweet salad cubed pickles
1 hard cooked egg, finely chopped

1 teaspoon sugar
½ teaspoon garlic, chopped
salt and pepper, to taste

MIX all ingredients until completely blended. Refrigerate at least two hours to blend flavors before serving.

Makes about 2 cups

Easy "Po' Folks" Salad Dressing

CAROLYN GOFF, Harnett County

"This is my mother's homemade salad dressing," Carolyn told me. "It's like French or thousand island."

1 cup mayonnaise

¾ cup buttermilk

½ cup catsup

1 to 2 teaspoons lemon juice

½ to ¾ cup sweet pickle relish or cubed pickles

BLEND THE mayonnaise, buttermilk, and catsup until smooth. Gradually stir in the lemon juice, tasting after 1 teaspoonful to see if you want to add more. Mix in the relish, again tasting after ½ cup to see if you want to add more. Refrigerate.

Makes about 3 cups

Easy Blue Cheese Salad Dressing

TREVA GREER *(from The Favorite Recipes of Beck's United Church of Christ)*, Davidson County

You can substitute Roquefort for the blue cheese. If you like a chunky texture, don't soften the blue cheese before you mash it. If you like a smooth texture, let it soften to room temperature before mashing it.

5 ounces blue cheese

1 cup sour cream

1 cup mayonnaise

garlic, crushed, optional

USE A FORK to mash the blue cheese into rough pieces. Set aside.

Combine the sour cream and mayonnaise. Blend thoroughly. Stir in the blue cheese. Season with garlic. Refrigerate.

Makes 2½ cups

Slaw Dressing

MRS. JOE BOYETTE, Sampson County

This recipe comes from Something Old - Something New from the Women's Club of Clinton, published in 1975, and somewhat unique in its presentation. Each cook handwrote her recipes, which were then copied into the book. Mrs. Boyette makes a note at the end of hers after she signs it, "1946," probably indicating the date she obtained it.

2 cups salad oil	*2 teaspoons paprika*
1 cup vinegar	*1 teaspoon celery salt*
½ cup sugar, optional	*2 scallions, finely chopped*
2 tablespoons mustard	*salt and pepper, to taste*

MIX ALL ingredients well. Let it stand overnight. The next day, strain out the onions and pour the dressing over shredded cabbage, which has been soaked in ice water for an hour, then drained. Put dressing on slaw one hour before serving.

Makes about 4 cups

Index